House Proud

House
Proud

Danielle Proud

NORTH LIGHT BOOKS

First published in North America
by North Light Craft
an imprint of F+W Publications, Inc.
4700 East Galbraith Road , Cincinnati, OH 45236
800-289-0963

fw
F+W PUBLICATIONS, INC.

First Published in Great Britain in 2006 by
Bloomsbury Publishing Plc, 36 Soho Square, London W1D 3QY
www.bloomsbury.com/danielleproud

A CIP catalogue record for this book is available from the British Library

ISBN 1-60061-062-5
978-1-60061-062-2

10 9 8 7 6 5 4 3 2 1

Printed in Singapore by Tien Wah Press

All papers used are natural, recyclable products made from wood grown in
sustainable, well-managed forests. The manufacturing processes conform to the
environmental regulations of the country of origin

Photography by Amelia Troubridge
Photographs on pages 62, 63,104,105,140,141,142,143,148, 200 by Sue O'Brien
Book Design: Here+There
Illustrations by Kate Simunek

acknowledgements

With thanks to the following companies:

Cole & Son
MANUFACTURERS OF HAND PRINTED
WALLPAPERS SINCE 1875

BERNINA®

learn to dream
everybody owns great images

LIBERTY
FURNISHINGS

MISSONI HOME

OSBORNE & LITTLE

This is my first book, so there are going to be a few …

Family
A huge thank you to my favorite people: my parents Michelle & Rhymer Rigby, my husband Alex and my brothers Rhymer and Grant. Jane, my new sister. Edward and Ulrike Proud and my new brother-in-law Hecky, who has helped so much with Idea Generation PR.

I'd also like to thank Peta, Issi, Sam and Molly for being such brilliant friends and gorgeous models.

This Book
Amelia Troubridge for her stunning photography and friendship. Mike Jones at Bloomsbury and Zia Mattocks for their extreme patience and direction. Style goddess Caz Hildebrand. My agent Simon Benham. Sarah Habershon for her wonderful illustrations. Jocasta Brownlee and Anya Rosenberg.

Elsewhere
Thank you to Tracey MacLeod and Peter Bennet Jones at KBJ Management and Tiger Aspect. William Miller. Partners in crime Tiffanie Darke and Kate Spicer. Susie Steiner and patchwork superstar Stephanie Pettengell. Nick Elliot for all his hard work.

At Topshop, hip kitties Caren Downie, Jo Faralley and Stephanie Fletcher. At The Guide, Tim, Daniel, the ladies I lunch with: Teri, Sarah, Becky; and my dear friend Richard Vine.

And
Kate and all at Proud Gallery for helping me hide furniture from my minimalist husband. Sarah Shotton and Tanya Von Moser for helping with my shoots. Cher for long-distance support and Greta Sani for the same. My surrogate mother Roberta Bird and last but by no means least Dom and Emma for their kindness and advice.

contents

individualize your home

*H*ouse Proud is a new kind of guide that will give you the confidence to find your own style and the skills to express it. The idea came to me while I was flipping through interior magazines full of designer cushions, tarted-up old chairs and fabulous wallpapered furniture – pieces that cost hundreds or thousands of dollars. Worse, these achingly expensive *objets* were part of a 'look' which, totaled up, would cost my annual salary.

The thought struck me afresh when I started looking for furniture for the house my husband and I were buying. I went to Habitat and Heal's, then checked out homeware boutique Mint, and also Paul Smith's collection with Cappellini. There was plenty that I wanted, especially in the latter (chairs covered in Verner Panton fabrics!), but prices – almost $400 for a single chair in Habitat and more like $2,000 in Paul Smith – were prohibitive. An eight-chair dining set from Mr Smith would set you back ten grand – and that's before you've bought the table.

Soon after this fruitless shopping trip, I was visiting a friend and saw similar chairs in a dusty old antique shop at $78 each. They needed new upholstery and a few scratches polishing out, but, with basic craft skills, I realized that I could create my own set and buy snazzy designer fabrics for the upholstery with the money I'd saved. Eight chairs uncannily similar to Paul Smith's for less than the cost of two from Habitat.

I've always preferred making something individual to buying mass-produced pieces. It adds a personal touch and is a good opportunity to reinvent, restore and be creative – not to mention brush up on the practical skills my mother's generation were so good at: choosing the fabric to reupholster mismatching dining chairs to make them into a set or adding appliqué to cover the holes in an old blanket, for example. In the postwar years, this need for imaginative reinvention was integral to our parents' homes; it's also what gave their places a heart, continuity and a sense of the owner – not something that can be said of flat-pack furniture.

While the 'make do and mend' ethos isn't relevant to us today – IKEA and eBay mean that decent, inexpensive homeware is within most people's reach – the same skills can be. This book is about reclaiming the know-how that has skipped our generation, and choosing to recycle and restyle – and value – the objects that we already own, or pieces that others have discarded which have crossed our path or caught our eye.

In the following pages I've used stacks of my mother's vintage scarves – gifts from my dad when they first started dating – to make cushions; I've wallpapered a boring 1980s chest of drawers that saw me through my college years to give it a fresh, designer look, and found uses for old toys and a tired-looking table found in a friend's loft. Every piece has a narrative and together they tell stories of the past, the present and, in their new guises, the future. They tell my story: in the first chapter, I used three of my 1960s print dresses – one of which I was wearing at the party where I first met my husband – to make oven gloves, aprons and an ironing board cover. Working these favorite dresses into such items, once they were too threadbare to wear, means I'm now surrounded by fabulous memories every time I step into the kitchen – not to mention able to amuse my friends and family with the tale of how the dress I pulled my husband in is now doing second duty as oven mitts.

I am probably a little predisposed to homecraft, having spent a chunk of my childhood in America in the 1970s, where my mother, who was very taken with folk art, taught me patchwork, needlepoint and stencilling. My father worked in marketing by day but would spend his evenings painstakingly restoring antique furniture and would enlist my polishing skills. This serves to illustrate that most craft skills are exceptionally easy to pick up, even for children. I had the knack of découpage and wood-staining, and was quite a talented needlewoman by the age of ten. So no excuses.

This book is packed with all sorts of crafts, many that children will want to help with. So next time you decide your pad needs an upgrade, instead of wincing at the cost of a reconditioned chair in *Elle Decoration*, swap the shop-bought trail for a cosy afternoon's creativity. Think about you and your family, what you like and what you have: three steps to making your home your own unique haven. Why not découpage the scratched old breakfast table with 1960s *Vogue* covers or photographs of your friends? Découpage involves sticking your pictures to a surface and varnishing over them, and can be done in an afternoon. Or make new lampshades for the children's bedroom from some leftover wallpaper. Cherry-pick from eras and influences – rebalance and remix them to make a style that is your own.

The processes involved are fabulously therapeutic and there's plenty to inspire you. Today craft is chic, sociable and a million miles away from those stringy 1970s macramé owl wall-hangings. Hip new designers are producing comic-book cushions, papier-mâché dogs covered with dollar bills and racy messages in cross-stitch. These are craft pieces that look more like art – and command art-like price tags – yet they aren't that hard to make. All the more reason to do it yourself.

Putting your own rooms together is easy – in fact, it's very similar to putting an outfit together, which you do every morning. So dig out your old postcards, scraps of fabric and whatever else you've collected, stop drooling over interior 'porn' and start injecting personality into your home.

Kitchen

coordination is the key to hip kitchens

oven gloves and tea cozy

Tea cozies and oven gloves are the soft furnishings of the kitchen – they're the quickest way to add a flash of color and update décor without much effort. Here I used some 1960s dresses that I'd worn to death when first dating my husband. They were falling to pieces, but I couldn't bear to throw them out. Making the remnants into something new is the perfect excuse for keeping treasured clothes, and by creating something useful for the kitchen you're surrounding yourself with the memories they hold. Make a few extra as chic homespun gifts for friends.

YOU WILL NEED

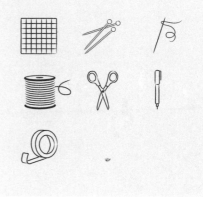

1 Some old cotton fabric – shirts, dresses or anything with large panels of fabric that don't have seams running through them. It's important to use cotton fabric rather than synthetic (which will melt) or wool (which will scorch). You'll need enough for eight glove shapes (that's the back and palm of each glove and the lining). I used a plain cloth on the inside, to conserve my prettier fabrics for other items around the kitchen.

2 Matching thread. If you're using mismatching cloth like I have, a neutral color is fine. Do use cotton – as above, synthetic thread will melt when it comes into contact with hot dishes.

3 Cotton batting – this is the woolly-looking padding that will stop your hands from burning, so go for something dense and about 1/2 in. thick.

4 Matching bias binding – to cover raw edges

5 Dressmaker's pins and a needle – a sewing machine is handy, but not essential

6 Fabric scissors – don't use paper scissors as these will be too blunt

7 Some old newspaper to make a pattern, plus a pen, tape measure and paper scissors

The method for oven mitts and tea cozies is very similar, so the instructions overleaf are for both. Making them together is much quicker than making them separately.

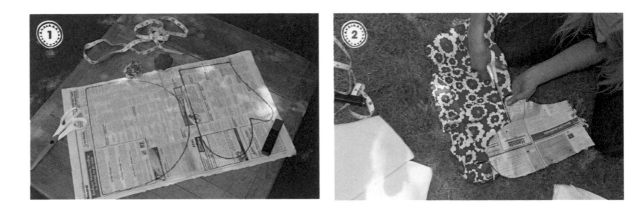

For the gloves, fold a sheet of newspaper in half and draw a mitten shape around your fingers and thumb, leaving at least 3/4 in. around the outside for movement. **[1]**

Keeping the paper folded (so that you get a left and right hand for the gloves), cut out the shape, snipping 1/4 in. outside the line you've drawn, all the way around to allow for the seam. Be sure to cut through both layers of paper.

Pin the paper patterns to the fabric that you want to use for the outer part of your gloves. Keep the pattern pieces in line with the grain or weave of the cloth – that is, parallel to the edge, or selvedge, of your fabric. To do this, fold the pattern in half lengthways to create a straight line down the center and align this with the grain of the fabric as you pin the pattern in place. Working with the weave of the fabric means that it won't skew and the edges won't stretch when you start sewing. You need two pieces of outer fabric for each hand. I used a 1960s floral print for one side of my gloves and an old checked shirt of my husband's for the other side. **[2]**

Cut four pieces of fabric for the lining – that's two for the left glove and two for the right – working in line with the weave of the fabric, as before.

Cut four pieces of cotton batting. This is what's going to stop your hands from burning, so it needs to be at least 1/2 in. thick.

To make the first glove, pin two pieces of outer material together, right sides facing, with a piece of batting on the outside of each. **[3]** Stitch around the glove shape, leaving the wrist end open. Trim the edges down to 1/8 in. from the seam. Turn it right sides out.

Pin the two lining pieces together, with right sides facing, and sew around the glove shape, l e a v i n g the wrist open, as before. Snip 'nips' along the curved seam you've just sewn to stop it from puckering. Then iron this seam open. Slot the lining inside the

padded outer piece of the glove. Pull the batting down firmly so the fit is snug.

Pin the bias binding around the bottom (wrist) edge of the glove, sandwiching in all the raw edges. Hand-sew this neatly in place, keeping your stitch line as close to the edge of the bias binding as possible and making sure you catch the binding in your seam on both sides. When you have sewn all the way around, fold the end of binding under and, overlapping where you started, stitch it down for a neat finish. Do the same for the other glove and you're done.

Fancy a cuppa?
Making a tea cozy uses the same method, except you only make one and you need to devise a shape that fits over your teapot, rather than a hand. Take a sheet of newspaper and draw then cut out a curved 'N' shape, an inch taller and wider than your teapot (mine is $9^3/4$ in. high, by 13 in. wide), with a straight line across the bottom. Using this as your pattern and working on the straight grain (parallel to the fabric edge) cut out two pieces of each of the following: outer fabric, lining fabric and batting. Pin the outer pieces together, right sides facing, with a piece of batting on either side. Sew along

the curved edge, leaving the bottom open. Trim the fabric to $1/8$ in. from the seam and turn right sides out.

Pin the lining pieces together, with right sides facing, then sew around the curved seam. Cut nips in the seam and iron it open. Slip the lining inside the outer piece. Sandwich the raw edges at the bottom with bias binding and sew it in place, as before.

Pat yourself on the back and decide what project to get onto next, or make more of these – you must have a friend who deserves such a stylish present.

retro apron

Shop-bought aprons tend to be huge 'one size fits all' sheet-like things – domestic togas, usually with idiotic slogans about the chef's inclinations emblazoned across the front. They're a far cry from the retro-chic fitted frills of 1950s Oxo ads or naughty Agent Provocateur pinnies.

Making your own apron is a must for any modern homemaker who finds cooking a perfect Hollandaise as important as looking saucy. And while you're at it, why not make matching pinnies for your little helpers – children will love having their own and they'll look too cute for words.

YOU WILL NEED _____

1   Approximately 1yard of fabric for an adult-size apron (you might well get two out of it if the fabric is very wide)
2   A patch of fabric for the pocket – a contrasting color or pattern looks good
3   Matching ribbon for the ties around your neck and waist
4   Bias binding or ribbon to match the pocket fabric
5   Matching cotton thread
6   Dressmaker's pins and a needle – a sewing machine is handy, but not essential
7   Newspaper, pen, tape measure and paper scissors to make the pattern
8   Fabric scissors

METHOD

Decide on the size you want your apron to be. I did this by holding a sheet of newspaper against my front and trimming it until I was happy with the shape. This is a good exercise for seeing what proportions suit you – it may even help with future fashion purchases – and it also makes you realize that even an apron can be flattering. I went for something pretty high at the front and finishing mid-thigh. **[1]**

On another piece of paper draw a pocket shape; this needs to be big enough to fit whatever you might use it for. Frankly, it's unlikely you'll put anything in it – what are kitchen surfaces for? – so go for a shape and fabric that look good. It's worth remembering that the eye will be drawn to wherever you position the pocket. Placing it just above the hips will be more flattering than if it's in line with your widest point. If you make the bottom of the pocket curved, rather than making it square or rectangular, you, like the pocket, will look less boxy.

Pin the newspaper patterns of the apron and pocket to the fabric, keeping them in line with the grain (parallel to the fabric edge or selvedge). Cut $1/2$ in. a round the outside of the apron shape, then cut out the pocket shape to the same size as your paper pattern. The $1/2$ in. extra on the apron is so that you can turn raw edges under to hide them. You don't need this side hem allowance on the pocket because you're going to trim it with binding or ribbon.

Work your way all around the apron folding the raw edges under twice and pinning them in place as you go. Iron this hem flat, then sew all the way around, keeping your stitches as close to the edge of the fold as possible, then iron again. The ironing is worthwhile – this sounds like a lot of ironing, but makes the difference between a professionally finished piece and something that looks like it came out of a badly taught Home Economics class. Put the apron to one side.

Pin ribbon or bias binding to the top of your pocket, sandwiching it around the raw edge. Iron it flat, then sew it in place. **[2]**

Now pin ribbon or bias binding around the curved edge of the pocket in the same way and pin the pocket in position on your apron front. Sew around this curved edge, attaching the pocket to the apron, then iron it flat.

Take four pieces of ribbon – two are for tying around your neck, the other two are to go around your waist. Fold both ends of each piece of ribbon under twice and iron them down. Sew down one of the ends of each piece of ribbon.

Pin the unsewn ends of two of the pieces of ribbon to the sides of your apron at the waist and sew these in place. **[3]**

Pin the unsewn ends of the other two pieces of ribbon to either side of the top of your apron so you can tie them around your neck. Sew these down, too, then fling it on. Now get cooking and bake something as tasty – and gateau-fabulous – as you're looking.

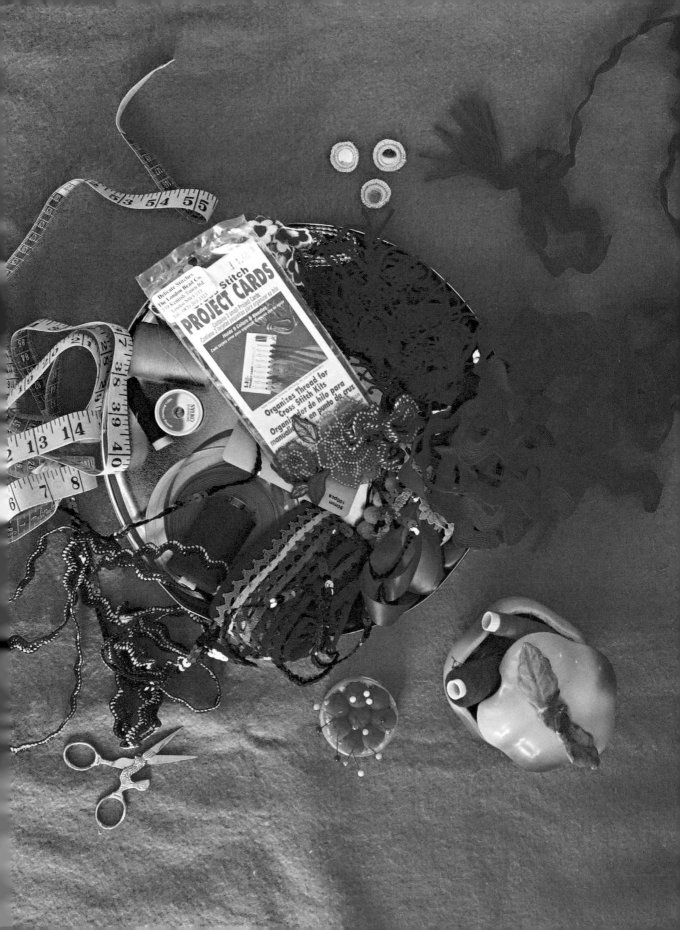

cushion covers with ponytail ribbons

Cushion covers are so simple to make. These will take around 40 minutes each – and less once you get into the swing of things. Start by forgetting plain and boring: the ribbon ties will add a carnival of color and are a great way to coordinate other fabrics and colors that you have going on in your kitchen. Kids will love choosing ribbons and naughty cats will play with them for hours. Plus, you'll have the satisfaction of realizing just how much retailers of soft furnishings mark up their own offerings. Get inspired and make different versions with mix-and-match fabrics.

YOU WILL NEED _____

1   A cushion pad the same size as your chair seat
2   Fabric – sufficient to wrap around your cushion pad with an inch to spare
3   A zipper 3 in. shorter than the width of your cushion pad
4   Matching thread
5   Dressmaker's pins and a needle
6   Sewing machine
7   Fabric scissors and a tape measure
8   A selection of ribbons – five or six strands for each corner (measure from the chair seat to the floor and add 1 in. to work out an approximate length for each strand)

METHOD

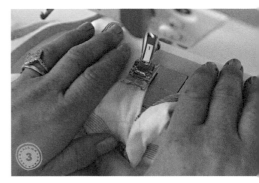

Measure your chair seat to decide the size you'd like your cushion to be. Mine are 11³/4 in. square. Between 9³/4 in. and 11³/4 in. square is pretty standard for a kitchen chair.

Cut two squares of fabric a half-inch smaller than you want your finished cushion to be. Making the cover a tad smaller will keep the cushion looking puffy. If you go bigger than the pad (which seems logical) your cushion will look like a satsuma in a sock. Sew around the outside of each square using zigzag stitch on your sewing machine.

Cut your ribbons and separate them into equal bundles. You need two bundles, one for each back corner of each of the cushion. Pile one end of each of the ribbons neatly on top of each other and stitch them together.

Place the right sides of your fabric together. Pin a bundle of ribbons to the two back corners a half-inch in from the sides. The lengths of ribbon should be hidden in between the two

fabrics, not hanging out. Starting ¹/4 in. from the edge, sew 1¹/2 in. of the back seam from each corner, securing the ribbons into the seam. The big hole left in center is where the zipper will go. **[1]**

Open the material out in front of you, with the wrong side facing up. Iron the seam allowance around the hole in the back seam. Pin your zipper into the hole, making sure that the ironed edges on the right side will meet when the zipper is closed. **[2]**

Undo the zipper and sew all the way around it, making sure you don't stitch over any rogue ribbons. Sew as close to the zipper teeth as you can for a neat finish. (Use a zipper foot, if you have one, to get as near to the teeth as possible.) **[3]**

Leaving the zipper open, pin then sew the remaining three sides of the cushion cover together, with right sides facing. Sew a few extra stitches at the start and finish of the seam to

secure. If you're hand-sewing, finish by tying a few knots in the thread.

Snip away the excess fabric diagonally across each corner and iron your seams open. This makes the cushion neat on the outside; if you don't, the seams will look bumpy. Turn the cover right sides out (by pulling it through the zipper hole), push your pad inside and tie the ribbons to the chair back.

Now snip the trailing ends of the ribbons to a length that you like and admire your work. Vibrant maypoles of color – and in no time at all. What were you waiting for?

charred chair
with a woven seat

Recycling is an exciting trend in interior design, allowing you to make a virtue out of being hip. Young designers are reclaiming discarded furniture, thrown-away carts and used computers, messing about with them and producing astonishing new items – all from junk that most of us would take to the dump.

The pioneers of creative recycling are changing perceptions of what is actually waste and redefining its value. Design group Committee have produced the eccentric 'Kebab' lamps, which have a stack of disused objects skewered down the center to make a stem; they look great – and sell for $4,000. Maarten Baas, a Dutch artist, burns furniture before sealing the charred remains with epoxy resin, producing equally stunning, similarly pricey results. Both are a good example of what's possible, just through reusing and creatively reinterpreting what we already have.

I'm not suggesting that you torch your grandmother's Louis XV chair – that would be stupid and could jeopardize your inheritance. But picking up something inexpensive and then experimenting with a few of the 'freestyle' ideas that litter interiors magazines is fun and a first step on the road to creating your own fantastic art pieces.

In fact, deconstruction is a lot easier than making something from scratch, and the techniques are often much simpler than the effect implies. It really is just as easy as changing the buttons on an old jacket – only the finished piece will be much more dramatic.

For this project, I bought a nineteenth-century chair at a local auction for $23. A few of the back struts were missing – the perfect invitation to deconstruct further and turn its imperfection into a design feature using macramé techniques (see page 88).

Your chair will obviously be a different design, so you just need to be flexible with your approach. Start by putting it where you'll walk past it a few times a day; after a couple of days you'll have a better sense of its proportions and will be brimming with creative vision for your own cutting-edge treasure.

YOU WILL NEED

For the charred chair

1 Chair
2 Fine-grade sandpaper and a damp cloth
3 Wood stain
4 Blow torch (they're very cheap from hardware stores/websites)
5 Mask and safety goggles
6 Latex or rubber gloves
7 Clear sealer
8 Epoxy resin and hardener (approximately 2 quarts in total should be plenty; do explain to your supplier what you're using it for, so you don't end up with the wrong kind).
9 Bowl for mixing resin
10 Two cheap decorator's paintbrushes, each around 3/4 in. wide
11 Hack saw
12 Material for découpage (optional)

For the chair seat

1 Macramé jute (try www.kingskountry.com, or nautical suppliers). For a large chair like this one you'll need around 200 yards in one or two colors. For a more natural look you can use seagrass, which you buy by the hank (500g) – about 15.5 yards.
2 Piece of dowelling 1/2 in. (12mm) in diameter and about 4 in. longer than the widest part of the chair frame
3 Large flat needle for weaving or an old wire coat hanger
4 Chalk

Sand the surface lightly using fine-grade sandpaper, then wipe over it with a damp cloth to remove all the dust.

Go outside, place the chair on a concrete surface or on the grass, miles from anything flammable (and certainly not next to the barbecue gas canister).

Using a small decorator's brush, paint the entire surface with a dark wood stain. Dark colors (such as walnut or ebony) look better with burnt sections, as there is little contrast, which makes the work look deliberate, rather than a mistake.

METHOD

Before you start, get into prayer position and chant, 'I am an artiste.' Not really. But it is worth taking a few points into account:

- In terms of design, your first hunch is usually right.
- Don't spend ages pondering on the details.
- Whenever something is labelled as art, it makes it sound important and scary. Just focus on trying out these techniques rather than creating 'art' – you'll find you enjoy the process more and you won't get too hung up on the end result.
- Less is more. A little embellishment, rather than taking a 'with bells on' approach, will always look better. You may decide that just one of these techniques will suit your chair. And you'd probably be right … I've never been accused of subtlety.

Decide which areas of your chair you want to burn – a couple of small places on the back tends to look good, as well as an edge or a strut here and there. Be careful that whatever you plan to do will not ruin the structure of the chair. I burnt away three struts, leaving plenty more to support the back of the chair. Burning the wood takes ages, so save a bit of time by sawing away the wood you want to

remove first, using a hack saw. Then all you need to do is char the edges.

Put on your safety goggles and, following the blow-torch manufacturer's instructions, carefully burn the edges of the sections that you have sawn away until they take on a charred appearance. Once you are happy with how it looks, allow the chair to cool completely. **[1]**

Wipe the edges of the sections that you've burnt and break off any weakened bits of charred wood. Spray the remaining charred edges with a clear sealing agent (such as Plasti-kote Clear Sealer). This is so you won't smear any dusty charred bits

with your paintbrush when you come to apply the epoxy resin and hardener. **[2]**

Now is the time to add any surface detail that you would like. I découpaged on a few pictures of birds and leaves in yellow and red to match the colors I used to weave the new seat (see pages 42–45 for découpage techniques). You may decide your chair doesn't need it.

Wearing your mask, goggles and latex gloves (trying not to think about how you look), mix the epoxy resin and hardener. Unlike paint drying in air, resin sets as a result of the chemical reaction that occurs when it is mixed with the hardener. Resin must be used

outside as the fumes are awful. GO STRAIGHT TO THE NEXT STEP, as the catalyst and resin begin working as soon as they are mixed.

Using a cheap 3/4 in. paint brush, apply a thick coat of resin to the sealed charred areas, then paint a thinner coat over the rest of the chair. Using more resin on the charred areas gives the weakened wood more strength.

Let the resin dry in a dust-free room, such as a garage. This will take several hours. Once it is hard to the touch and with no sticky patches, leave the chair in a warm room or in the sun for 2–3 days. This is called post curing and it toughens the resin.

Weaving the chair seat

Once the resin is completely hard you can start weaving the chair seat. Weaving is a fabulously hard-wearing alternative to upholstery and, thanks to the array of colors and materials available, the results can be modern, striking and unique. The method I used here is the traditional alternate method. As I'd burnt the back of this chair I thought a traditional approach for the seat would be better, in terms of design balance, than anything more haphazard.

Mark the center of the seat frame with chalk, on the front and back edge; this is where you'll begin weaving. Starting in the middle ensures that you get the same number of strands on either side, so the end result is balanced.

Weave from front to back first. Tie the macramé jute to the front of the frame, with a secure knot on the underside. Then, neatly bundle up the rest of the length of the cord, or wrap it around a piece of card to make it easier to work with.

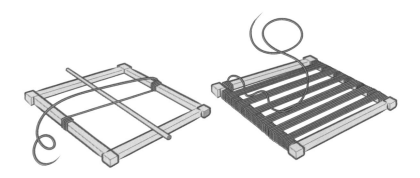

Place the dowelling across the center of the frame (from left to right), so it's at right angles to the direction you'll be working in. When you start weaving, you should pass each strand over the top of the dowelling as you go. The dowelling eases the tension of the cords to make it easier when you come to weave across the chair seat.

Loop the macramé jute four times around the front of the frame, then take it to the back, on the underside of the frame. Loop it around the back of the frame four times, then return it to front top side of the frame. The four loops around the chair frame at each end create the spaces between each group of cross-strands. If your chair

frame has a wider front and narrower back, broaden the coverage at the front by doing five loops instead of four on every alternate round.

Go straight from front to back for five rounds (going from front to back on the underside and back to front on the top side). Keep the lines of cord neat and right next to each other with no gaps between them.

Repeat this method (four loops around the front, then four loops around the back, then five rounds from front to back), working from the center out to each side, bearing in mind you need the same number of strands on each side of your halfway marks. You should finish

the weaving at each side with four loops at the front and back of the frame. Then remove the dowelling and get ready to weave from side to side.

This is the same method as before, except now you're going to work across the frame from side to side, using the second color of macramé jute. Start at the back corner of the frame, rather than in the center as you did with front. (You can work from front to back if you prefer – it makes no odds.) You'll need a large needle to pull the strands through – or you can fashion one out of an old wire coat hanger. I used a needle made from a coat hanger for the bulk of this weaving, then just pulled the jute through by hand when I was very close to the front and it got more fiddly. [3]

Secure the macramé jute to the side of the frame, with a knot on the underside. Loop four times around the side of the frame, then take the cord across to the opposite side, weaving under the first five strands, and over the next five strands, and so on, before looping four times around the opposite side of the frame. You can use the dowelling to lift alternate sections – some weavers recommend this as it makes getting the needle from side to side quicker.

Go back on the underside, weaving under and over, following the path of the cord from the other side. Weave five rounds in this way and repeat the four loops. Continue in this manner until you get to the end. Use reef knots underneath to secure the loose ends.

Sit in your chair and have a cuppa or watch TV. You've earned it.

recycling bag

This recycling bag is so quick to make that you should tag it onto the end of another sewing project, like the ironing board cover (page 50). It'll be as chic and frivolous as the fabric you choose. More importantly, it's genuinely useful – it'll turn the unsightly avalanche of shopping bags under the sink into a fountain of loveliness, and hopefully encourage everyone in the house to recycle. Sure, it's a drop in the ocean in terms of the 10 billion or more shopping bags used in the US every year, but you have to start somewhere. What could be more appropriate than a recycling bag made out of an old shirt or your leftover curtain fabric?

YOU WILL NEED _____

1   A piece of fabric, 25$\frac{1}{2}$ in. square
2   A yard of ribbon at least $\frac{1}{4}$ in. wide or macramé jute
3   11$\frac{3}{4}$ in. of $\frac{1}{4}$ in. elastic (use white with pale fabric, black with dark)
4   Tape measure and tailor's chalk or fabric marker pen
5   Fabric scissors
6   Dressmaker's pins, a safety pin and a needle; a sewing machine if you have one
7   Matching thread

METHOD

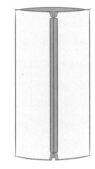
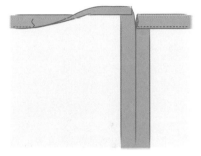

Cut a piece of fabric 25$\frac{1}{2}$ in. square and zigzag around the raw edges, using a sewing machine.

Fold the fabric in half with right sides facing and pin the longest sides together, leaving the top and bottom open.

Measure 1 in. in from the top and bottom and mark these positions on the side seam. Leaving the 1 in. at the top and bottom unsewn, sew $\frac{1}{4}$ in. in from the edge along the length of your fabric to make a tube (see above, left).

Iron the seam open. Then fold and iron back a $\frac{1}{4}$ in. seam allowance on the unsewn sections at the top and bottom (see above, center).

Fold the whole top edge of the 'tube' under twice, using no more than $\frac{1}{4}$ in. fabric in the fold. Iron and sew down as close to the fold line as you can. When you get to the side seam, secure the seam allowance that you previously folded back and ironed with a line of stitching.

Fold this whole section under, to the point where the side seam finishes, and sew all the way around to create a channel (see above, right).

Repeat the previous two steps to create a channel along the bottom edge of the bag.

Attach a safety pin to one end of the elastic and pull it through the channel at the bottom of the bag (pin the other end of the elastic near the entrance to the channel to make sure it doesn't follow, or you'll have to start again). Once you've pulled the safety pin all the way around the channel and out the other side, secure the two ends of elastic together with a few stitches. This creates the bottom of the bag where you will pull the shopping bags from.

Now attach the safety pin to the piece of ribbon or jute and pull this through the top channel. Tie the two ends in a knot and hang your new recycling bag on the back of your kitchen door – out of reach of playful paws.

transfer-print roller blinds

There's no shame in buying roller blinds. Why bust a gut making something that's too boring to wow your friends when countless professionals will make them to measure for you, at very little expense. But when you buy, do buy plain – as in blank canvas – because there's bags of room for creative improvement to make a window dressing that people will notice. Transfer printing is the perfect way to add originality and rebel in a low-maintenance way against the plain-and-same high street. It's quick and easy and you don't need any skill, except a gentle touch for handling flimsy transfers. What better way to put your own stamp on that sleek, modern and utterly identikit kitchen? I mean, who doesn't have granite work surfaces and a wok burner these days?

YOU WILL NEED _____

1   Blinds – they must be made from a material that can withstand the heat of an iron on the silk setting, so you should check with the manufacturer, or ask them to send you a scrap of fabric to test yourself. Don't ignore this point, as some fabrics will melt.
2   Camera for photos or other images
3   Lazertran Inkjet Textile Transfer Paper, or equivalent product
4   Inkjet (not laser) printer (or go to a photocopy shop)
5   Iron and ironing board
6   To put up the blinds: a drill, spirit level, yard stick, pencil
7   Scissors

METHOD

Blinds clip easily in and out of the brackets, so fit these first and check that the blind hangs straight before you get on with the fun part. Your blind should come with detailed instructions on how to put it up, but here are a few tips:

• Get your dad to do it, or at least ask him to help you. Men get a sense of achievement out of even the most mundane DIY tasks – really, you're doing them the favor.

• Double- and triple-check your measurements – including how far the blind will stick out from the window frame.

• Measuring from the ceiling or window frame often gives iffy results, as ceilings aren't as straight as you'd assume they should be. Before you start drilling, check the positioning of your brackets by drawing a light pencil line with a yard stick between where you have marked your two bracket points and check this with a spirit level. When you drill, make sure you hold the drill at an exact right angle to the wall.

• Once you're happy with the positioning, unclip the blind, fire the old man and get onto the fun part.

Find your images. I have a wonderful collection of mismatching plates, cups and saucers found in yard sales and thrift stores. These were a little out of step with this modernized kitchen, but perfect for making into transfers to polka-dot across the white expanse of these new blinds. Weaving traditional objects into a modern context challenges familiar perceptions. What was old hat, even chintzy, becomes fresh and unusual. I played around with different combinations to see which looked good together, then photographed each piece separately to create individual transfers. You can use anything picture-wise, from holiday snaps or photos of flowers in your garden to swirly Arts and Crafts patterns that you've traced or made up yourself. Just consider the space you want to cover. Plates work well, as they give the effect of a large-scale print, without the hassle of matching up lots of transfer sheets. [1]

Download your photos and print the images onto a sheet of Lazertran Inkjet Textile Transfer Paper using (you guessed it) an inkjet printer. The transfer comes out in reverse, so use the mirror-image mode when printing – this is especially relevant if there are words in your picture.

Place your printouts to one side for half and hour so the ink dries completely, then carefully cut out the images you want to use. At this stage the transfer will look lighter than your original image because of the milky color of the glue in the paper; as soon as you apply heat, the glue melts and become clear, so the colors appear dense. [2]

If, like me, you haven't created a pattern that needs to be joined up at specific points, play around with your transfers to see which look best together. [3] Stand back to see how the images look from a distance, as this is how you'll see them most of the time.

It's well worth getting a second opinion. Make yourself a quick sketch so you don't forget.

Iron the blind fabric at the hottest temperature it can withstand to warm it up. **[4]**

Lay your transfer face down on the right side of the blind fabric. Applying consistent pressure, iron the back of the transfer in circular motions to distribute the heat evenly. Do this for between 60 and 90 seconds for a small image and 90 to 120 seconds for a larger image (like my plates). While you are ironing, concentrate on using the center of the iron and pay particular attention to the edges of the transfer. **[5]**

Allow the fabric and transfer to cool, then gently peel away the backing paper from one corner or edge, using steady pressure. If the image starts to pull away from the fabric, iron for a little longer or increase the iron's temperature. If you are applying more than one image, as I have, iron all of the images in place first, before removing the backing paper.

Slot the blind back into the brackets, stand back and admire your work. A decorative masterpiece that is miles more charming than a boring block of wishy-washy white.

NB: For future care of your transfer-print blind, always iron with baking parchment laid over the prints to protect them. Most blinds are wipe-clean and don't require washing, but if yours is washable, wash at a maximum temperature of 100°F (40°C) and do not tumble dry.

découpage kitchen table

Découpage produces astounding, professional results for very little outlay and effort. It is nothing more complicated than cutting out some pictures, sticking them on to a surface, then finishing with a varnish or lacquer, but the results look like weeks of painstaking hand-painting. The word découpage comes from the French 'découper', which means to cut out.

Early examples date back to twelfth-century Asia, but in Europe, the craft became popular in the seventeenth and eighteenth centuries, when demand for hand-painted furniture outstripped supply, making the real thing eye-wateringly expensive. Ladies of the day, not to be thwarted by what must have been the contemporary equivalent of the waiting list for a Chloé handbag, took matters into their own hands and began collaging images onto furniture to give the impression of hand-painting. At first, this sleight of hand was seen as a poor man's art, but it soon became recognized in its own right.

You can découpage wood, painted walls and even melamine (just paint with special melamine paint first); and the images can be anything from traditional prints to modern art. I have even used pictures from 1970s *Playboy* magazines – probably not quite what découpaging's Georgian practitioners had in mind when they first refinished a table – but it demonstrates how to, quite literally, drag a traditional craft into the noughties. It also offered a rare glimpse of my husband showing an interest in my work.

YOU WILL NEED

1 Table
2 Medium-grade sandpaper or a piece of broken glass with a straight edge and some fine-grade sandpaper
3 Thick gloves
4 Damp cloth
5 Scissors
6 Soft paintbrushes
7 Paint or wood stain
8 Pictures, old postcards, scraps of wrapping paper
9 Spray mount adhesive (try 3M Pro-Spray which is water-based; solvent-based adhesives are harmful to your health and the environment and should be avoided if possible)
10 Quick-drying clear wood varnish (again, go for something environmentally friendly, such as a water-based varnish from Ecos Paints, and consider the finish – matt and satin, on the whole, will look classier than gloss)
11 Shellac (available from art or craft stores)

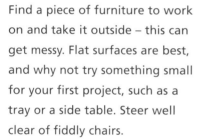

Find a piece of furniture to work on and take it outside – this can get messy. Flat surfaces are best, and why not try something small for your first project, such as a tray or a side table. Steer well clear of fiddly chairs.

Remove any knobs. Then, if you are working on wood, scrape off the old varnish wearing thick gloves. **[1]** You can do this either by sanding with medium-grade sandpaper or by scraping across the surface with the straight edge of a piece of broken glass – this is a trick my dad taught me and it takes infinitely less time than sanding. (If you are working on a painted surface, just sand enough to roughen it, so that a new layer of paint will stick. Wipe with a damp cloth, then repaint.) **[2]**

When you've finished sanding, blow off the dust, then give the surface a quick wipe with a damp, not wet, cloth. **[3]** Dampening the wood makes the grain rise. Then sand with fine sandpaper to a smooth finish.

If you want to stain the wood When the surface is dry, apply the wood stain using swift, even strokes in line with the wood grain. (If the surface is not wood, work in one direction.) I used ebony wood stain mixed with varnish. **[4]**

Cut out the pictures you want to use. Anything can work here, from vintage wallpapers to comic books or botanical illustrations. Nail scissors are great for cutting out intricate shapes, like the spindly legs and beaks on these birds I used. [5]

Paint your images on both sides with a thin layer of shellac. This is a quick-drying yellowish resin that seals the paper. If you don't use it, the paper will stretch and ripple when you varnish it. [6]

When the shellac and painted surfaces are completely dry, spray the back of your images with spray mount. This makes them sticky but moveable, so you can play around and decide where they look best. I started off with a whole flock of birds fluttering across this table (which looked awful) before realizing that, as in most cases, less is more.

When you have decided on your design, press the images down firmly, making sure they are completely flat. If you've moved them around a lot, you may need to spray on a little more adhesive to fix them. [7]

Using a paintbrush, apply matt or satin varnish over the whole surface, including the images, then leave it to dry. [8]

When the varnish is completely dry, apply eight more coats at intervals, waiting for each coat to dry completely before slicking on the next. The more coats you paint on, the smoother your finish will be. In Victorian times between 30 and 40 coats were common – but then people were trying to disguise the process.

shopping bags

This is the perfect project for that gorgeous length of fabric that you've left gathering dust for two years in the cupboard (don't kid yourself, it's still in there). Shopping bags are quick to make and require no technical skill. By making your own you'll have something original and chic. You'll also eliminate the need for ugly plastic bags, which take a thousand years to biodegrade and drag a lady's image into the gutter.

YOU WILL NEED

1   Fabric – half a yard of 42-45 in-wide fabric (normal fabric width) is fine for a 14 x 12$\frac{1}{4}$ in. bag
2   Matching cotton thread
3   Tape measure
4   Dressmaker's pins and a needle – a sewing machine is handy, but not essential
5   Fabric scissors

METHOD

Cut two pieces of fabric 15$\frac{3}{4}$ in. by 13 in. Remem-ber to cut in line with the grain of the fabric (that's parallel to the selvedge). This measurement is for a finished bag measuring 14 in. by 12$\frac{1}{4}$ in. wide. For the record, the break-down of this measure-ment follows: 15$\frac{1}{4}$ in. (14 in. length plus $\frac{1}{4}$ in. seam allowance at the bottom and 1 in. allowance for the hem at the top); 13 in. width (12$\frac{1}{2}$ in. plus $\frac{1}{4}$ in. seam allowance on each side). Feel free to make a different size, but do use the same seam allowances.

Turn the top edge of both pieces of fabric under by $\frac{1}{4}$ in. and iron , then turn these pressed folds under again by $\frac{1}{2}$ in. Iron, then stitch each one down – you've just created the hems for what

will be the top edge of the bag. Place the right sides of the fabric together and pin the sides and bottom of your bag together. Stitch a line $1/8$ in. from the edge.

Trim down the raw edge, so it is a $1/4$ in. from your stitch line, and cut a diagonal line across the corners, so excess fabric won't bunch up inside the seam you are about to sew.

Turn the bag right side out. Iron the seams flat, so the fabric is no longer 'dipping' in towards the first seam, then iron the bag flat on each side. I know it sounds like a lot of fussing, but ironing at these stages makes the difference between an amateur and a professional finish.

Working on what will be the outside of the bag (the right side of the fabric), top stitch around the sides and bottom of

the bag, $1/4$ in. in from the edge. This sandwiches in your first seam, eliminating untidy edges inside the bag. It's important to use a French seam for something like this, as it's more durable than a normal seam. [1]

The handles are very simple to make. A finished length of $29^{1}/2$ in. long and 1 in. wide is ideal for slinging over your shoulder or carrying in your hand, but not dragging on the floor. Cut two strips $30^{1}/4$ in. long by 3 in. wide: $30^{1}/4$ in. ($29^{1}/2$ in. length plus $3/4$ in. seam allowance); 3 in. (double the width, 2 in., as it's folded, plus $3/4$ in. seam allowance).

Fold each piece in half length-ways, so the wrong side of the fabric is facing you. Sew one short end of each piece, $1/4$ in. in from the edge. Then sew down the long sides, again $1/4$ in. in from the edge.

Using a slim ruler or paintbrush or similarly long object with a blunt end, poke the sewn end all the way back through the tubes of fabric. When you have turned them right sides out, iron them flat, so that the seams are in the center of the handles.

Turn the unsewn ends under twice and iron. Pin the ends of the handles onto your bag, about 4 in. in from the sides; make sure you pin them into the hem where the fabric is double thickness, as this gives the handles extra strength. Sew a square around the ends of the handles, then sew an 'X' through each one on both sides. [2 and 3]

Now hit the craft store for embroidery, crystals, ribbons and trim to embellish your bag.

covered books

Covering raggy-edged cookbooks and recipe files is remarkably satisfying. Use wrapping paper, bits of fabric or leftover wallpaper to coordinate with the walls. As with many crafts, it's worth doing a stack at a time. After the first one you'll have the knack and you'll be able to whiz through the rest in minutes. While you're at it, cover some blank notebooks – these make the perfect standby present for forgotten birthdays.

YOU WILL NEED

1 Hardback book
2 Large piece of paper that fits all the way around the book you want to cover with at least 2 in. to spare all round
3 Water-based spray mount, such as 3M Pro-Spray (do go for a water-based spray mount, rather than a solvent-based one, as these are harmful to your health and the environment)
4 Double-sided sticky tape
5 Roll of clear sticky-back plastic
6 PVA glue
7 Pen
8 Metal ruler
9 Craft knife
10 Scissors

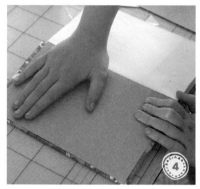
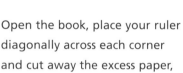

METHOD

If the book you're covering has a dust jacket with pleasing typography, cut out the title so that you can glue it to the front and spine of your new cover.

Lay the covering paper wrong side up on your work surface and place your book open in the center. Draw around it and mark the spine. Using your ruler, draw a line 2 in. outside the book outline and cut out along this line. Spray the wrong side of the paper with spray mount.

Place double-sided sticky tape down the length of the spine, then around the four edges of the front and back of the book cover, leaving the backing on the tape. Remove the tape backing from the spine only and carefully place the spine of your book on the paper, in between the spine markings that you drew when outlining the book.

Close the book, front side down then remove the tape backing on the back cover. **[1]** Hold the paper up and gently smooth from the spine across the back cover, so it sticks firmly.

Open the book, place your ruler diagonally across each corner and cut away the excess paper, to miter the corners. **[2]**

Cut a 'V' shape on either side of the spine, so you can fold the paper around the cover. Place double-sided sticky tape around the four edges of the inside of the back cover, remove the backing and fold the paper in. Flip the book over and repeat the above for the front cover.

Cut a piece of sticky-back plastic big enough to go all the way around the book and fold over the edges. Mark the center and gently peel off the backing paper to this point. Place the spine in the center, and smooth the plastic across the front and back of the book, as you did

with the paper. The plastic is repositionable, so if you get air bubbles, peel it back and try again. Miter the corners, as you did with the paper, cut 'V' shapes on either side of the spine and fold the plastic over the edges of the cover.

Pinch together the plastic and paper 'V' shapes sticking out of the spine of the book, then trim to about $1/4$ in. and add a lick of glue. **[3]** Open the book as far as it will go so that you can tuck the flap into the spine with your little finger or a pencil.

Cut a piece of colored paper $1/4$ in. smaller than the inside of the book cover and stick it down with double-sided sticky tape. **[4]** Voila, you have a flashy new book.

ironing board cover

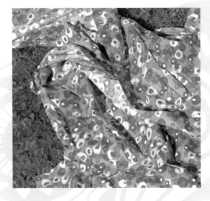

Why shouldn't even the most mundane domestic objects be glamorous? Ironing boards take up a lot of space and, for that reason alone, they should be top of your 'in need of transformation' hit list. With a little imagination and a yard and a half of decent fabric you can change one of these bleakly utilitarian and functional beasts into a fashion statement that looks better out of the closet than in it. It'll make ironing a whole lot more bearable, too.

YOU WILL NEED

1 1^1/$_2$ yard 100% cotton fabric (don't use anything other than cotton, as you need fabric that can withstand the heat of an iron)
2 Thin foam 3 in. longer than your ironing board
3 A piece of Bondaweb the length of your ironing board (Bondaweb is a fusible webbing that sticks to your fabric, and once you peel off the paper backing it will bond another fabric to the other side. You can get it from a fabric store)
4 3 yards of 1inch-wide bias binding that matches your fabric
5 Approximately 3.5 yards thin cord
6 Baking parchment for making your pattern (any paper will do, but parchment comes on a roll, so you won't need to stick lots of sheets together to get the length of an ironing board)
7 Dressmaker's pins, medium-sized safety pin and a needle – a sewing machine is handy, but not essential
8 Matching thread
9 Fabric scissors
10 Tailor's chalk or fabric marker pen
11 Iron and ironing board

METHOD

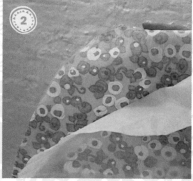

Place the ironing board upside down on a sheet of baking parchment or other similar light paper. Draw around the outline of the ironing board and cut out the shape.

Pin this pattern to the wrong side of your fabric (in line with the grain – that's parallel to the selvedge). Draw a dotted line on the fabric, 2 in. larger than the pattern all the way around, and cut along this dotted line, using sharp scissors.

Cut a piece of Bondaweb and thin foam 1¹/₂ in. bigger than your paper pattern.

Place the Bondaweb, rough side down (and paper side up), in the center of the back of your fabric. Don't put it on the patterned side of your fabric or you will have to start again. With your iron on the cotton setting, slowly iron the back of the paper, so that the sticky stuff has time to melt and fuse to your fabric. [1]

Once you're happy that the Bondaweb has stuck, allow it to cool for a few minutes, then peel the paper backing off. [2]

The wrong side of your fabric will now feel a little 'soapy'. Place the thin foam over this 'soapy' Bondaweb-ed area, flip it over and iron on the right side of the fabric. The heat will go through the fabric and fuse the other side of the Bondaweb to the foam. Don't iron the foam – it'll melt instantly. [3]

Fold your bias binding in half and iron down the fold.

Starting at the center of the straight edge, pin the bias binding around the perimeter of the ironing board cover, sandwiching the raw edge inside the fold. Catch the very edge of the foam in the binding, but just a little – too much foam inside this channel will make it tricky to pull the cord through. Turn the binding under twice at each end for a neat finish.

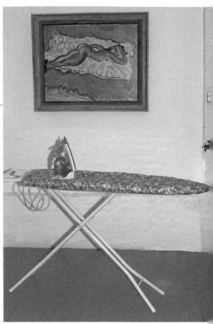

Sew all the way around the inside edge of the bias binding. It's worth doing this slowly, as you need to make sure you're catching the binding on both sides and keeping your seam line no less than 1/4 in. from the edge of the fabric – any less and you won't be able to squeeze the cord through the channel to secure your ironing board cover to the board. [4]

Singe the end of the cord with a lighter (assuming it's a synthetic material – most are) and pinch it, then attach a safety pin to the end. Gently shimmy the safety pin all the way through the channel; do this slowly. The reason I suggest melting the end is because cord frays easily – it's most annoying if you've already pulled it three-quarters of the way around the ironing board shape and the safety pin becomes detached.

Once you pull the safety pin out of the other side of the channel (congratulations!), place your new cover over your ironing board and pull both ends of the cord until it fits snugly over the top of the board. Tie the cords together underneath to secure.

Phew, at least that's a little more cheer put into the tedious task of ironing ... Which actually, once you click on the TV or a Red Hot Chilli Peppers album, makes you feel that a bout of domestic slavery isn't so bad after all.

acrylic cookbook stand

Thermoplastics, such as acrylic, become pliable when they're heated, meaning you can bend them into fabulous objects like this 1970s-style cookbook stand that shields pages from bolognaise and curry splatters. Ideal for those gourmets who believe that if you haven't trashed the kitchen then you're not putting your heart into it. A great mother's day gift, too. Watch her face light up when you don't give her a gift pack of toiletries.

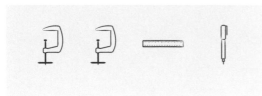

YOU WILL NEED _____

1 Sheet of acrylic – 17³/4 in. x 31¹/4 in. is fine for Moro / Jamie / Nigella fans (this measurement is the width of a cookbook open, by a little less than three times the length)
2 Heat gun (inexpensive in hardware stores, but you'll probably find a friend's dad has one tucked away)
3 Narrow piece of wood, 1 in. thick by 1 yard long, and a couple of chairs to balance it between
4 2 clamps
5 Ruler
6 Pen to mark the acrylic

METHOD

The idea is to bend the plastic into a slanted 'N' shape that you slot your cookbook into to hold it at a reading angle. Mark your acrylic for the three bends required. The first line across the acrylic should be 10½ in. from the top, the second 3¼ in. from the first line and the third 10 in. from the second line. [1]

Place the plank of wood between two chairs. Accurately line up the markings for your first bend with the edge of the plank, and clamp it in place.

Using even strokes, heat along this line with the heat gun, which is like an extra-hot hairdryer. [2] The plastic will slowly start to bend as it

becomes pliable. After ten minutes, gently press the plastic at the bottom edge – well away from the heated line. This gives more leverage and stops you from burning your hands. If it bends easily, very gently press with even pressure on both sides, so the acrylic bends at a 90 degree angle (in line with the edge of the plank of wood). The trick with any plastic is not to stress it. When it's hot enough, it bends with a feather-like touch. When it's not ready, you strain the plastic causing ugly stress lines that you cannot remove, so take your time.

Leave the bent acrylic until it is completely cool, then remove the clamp and piece of acrylic.

Turn the piece of wood, so the thin edge is facing toward the sky, and clamp on the acrylic ready for your second bend. Bear in mind that for this bend you'll just be folding the acrylic in a 'U' shape, down the other side of the plank. The width of the plank creates the gutter for your recipe books to rest in. [3]

Once this bend is completely set and cooled, remove the clamp and line up your third bend line with the edge of the plank. This bend needs to be around 30 degrees, but just do it by eye – really it just needs to be at an angle suitable for propping the book up. Wait until your stand is completely cool, then jump in with the messiest meal going.

Dining room

entertain the troops in style

wallpapered glass cabinet

Making a statement with a single papered wall is over. Yes, now it's two walls minimum, and to raise an eyebrow you'll have to wallpaper the furniture. Seriously, decorating the inside of a glass-fronted cabinet is the height of understated glamour – like having a fancy silk lining inside a plain black jacket. And, as you use so little paper, it costs next to nothing, so fans of Cole & Son's hand-gilded collections can breathe a collective sigh of relief. Papering is surprisingly easy to do – just follow a couple of simple rules when picking your furniture. Then, once you're satisfied with this cabinet, raise the bar and try wallpapering a chest of drawers (page 152).

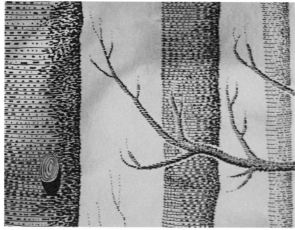

YOU WILL NEED _____

1   A glass-fronted cabinet – it's important that you pick one with a removable back (generally, this will be a nailed-on piece of plywood that you can easily lever off with a screwdriver). These are easy to come by, just start casually looking (eBay, markets, junk shops) and when something grabs you, snap it up.
2   Black gloss paint and paintbrush
3   Soft pasting brush
4   Wallpaper and wallpaper paste
5   Screwdriver with a flat end
6   Hammer
7   Fine sandpaper and soft cloth
8   Nails (3/4 in., no bigger)
9   Craft knife
10 Masking tape
11 Paint scraper

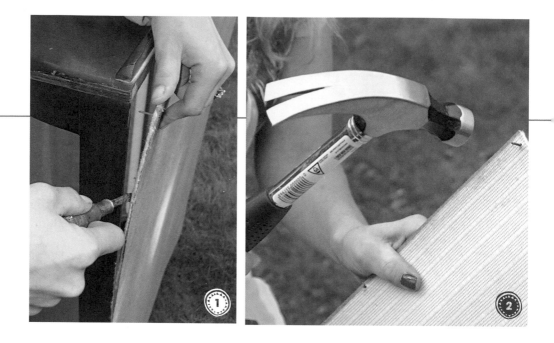

Remove the glass shelves – they should just slide out – and put them to one side.

Remove the wooden back of the cabinet. To do this, starting at one of the top corners, wedge the flat end of the screwdriver between the frame and back, just above each nail, and lever. Work all the way around and take off the back. [1]

The back will have a lot of nails sticking up, so lightly tap the pointy ends with a hammer to push them out the other side, then throw them away. Place the back to one side. [2]

Sand the cabinet lightly, to prep it for painting, then wipe the dust away with a soft cloth.

Using masking tape, mask off the glass so you don't end up covering it with paint.

Paint the cabinet using even strokes in line with the wood grain. I went for a black gloss paint to get the high-shine look of lacquer. You will probably need to apply two coats, so leave it to dry thoroughly after each one. [3]

NB: When you leave the cabinet to dry, rest the open door on something stable – like a couple of bricks – because without the weight of the back for balance, even a light breeze will send your cabinet crashing to the ground (this happened to me and here you're looking at my second attempt).

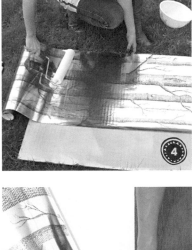

Apply a thin coat of wallpaper paste to the wrong side of a length of paper, then stick it squarely to the back piece of the cabinet. You can smooth it out from the center using either a clean paint roller or your hands, but don't overdo it. As the paste dries, wavy or bumpy bits tend to flatten out, as the moisture in the paste evaporates. [4]

Cut off the end of the paper using a sharp craft knife for a neat edge. [5] Apply more widths of wallpaper in the same way, as necessary, until the back of your cabinet is fully papered. Make sure you line up the pattern correctly with each adjacent piece and that the edges fit together without gaps.

While the back is drying, scrape any paint off the glass. That's assuming there is any (if you were careful with painting and masked the glass off, you'll have saved yourself this job). [6]

Using new nails, replace the back, then carefully slot the glass shelves back in. Smugly fill with martini glasses, a cocktail shaker and other such accoutrements that hint at a lifestyle befitting your glitzy furniture.

finding furniture

Finding decent pieces of furniture can become a wild goose chase. For the best markets, auction houses and other ideas for where to source furniture, flick straight to Resources on page 220.

What to look out for

- Choose pieces that are a fundamentally sound and avoid anything with cracks in the frame.
- Don't worry about loose joints, as these can easily be reglued – do this after stripping off old varnish or paint and before you commence the revamp.
- Pick out attractive shapes – an exterior or finish can be changed, a clunky shape can't.
- Large missing sections of veneer are a hassle – steer clear. Smaller patches can be levelled off with wood filler and stained, or découpaged.
- Surface imperfections, such as scratches and gouges, can be repaired with filler, then sanded. Ask for advice in your local hardware store.
- Layers of paint can be 'dipped and stripped' commercially. This is the only practical method for pieces with carved ornamentation or spindles, though it uses a lot of chemicals and is not great for the environment. Flatter pieces can be sanded by hand, or you can invest in an electric sander.
- Be strict about your budget when you hit the auction houses; it's easy to overbid and you won't like your treasure half as much once you get it home if you got carried away buying it.

peacock mirror-top table

This piece should have had pride of place in London's Biba store forty years ago – it would have fitted in perfectly with the 1930s glamour, potted palms and moody colors. Art Deco is the ideal era to plunder for dining rooms – it screams party-girl decadence and its geometric elegance is easy to mimic, thanks to mirrored tiles coming in big squares ready to fix. Here, I covered the top of a small side table. Don't feel restricted to tabletops, though, as you can cover any surface with straight edges including the inside of cupboards or sideboards. The peacock feathers are varnished on to add a little eccentric charm.

YOU WILL NEED

1 A piece of furniture to work on
2 Rectangular mirrored tiles (see the stockist list on page 219 – there's not a million places that do them)
3 PVA glue
4 Craft knife
5 Thin piece of card (for applying glue)

For the peacock feathers
6 2 peacock feathers
7 Spray-on clear craft sealant (Plasticote is good)
8 Spray mount (try water-based 3M Pro-Spray)
9 Varnish (try a water-based one, such as Earthborn, which isn't bad for your health or the environment)
10 Paintbrush

My table didn't have a top when I started, so my delightful assistant Nick cut a piece of MDF (medium-density fibreboard) to fit, applied glue to the frame, then laid the new top in place and nailed it down. You probably won't need to do this, but in the unlikely event of you picking up a topless table, rest assured that mirrored tiling on a cheap base is possibly the chicest remedy for the situation. [1]

Measure the surface of your table and work out how many sheets of tiles will fit on the top. You can't cut through the middle of the tiles (they're too small) and it won't look good if you try, but you can cut complete strips off the edge of a sheet. When I was fitting mine, I realized that even this wouldn't make them fit, but turning a single row of tiles sideways to go in the middle made a perfect fit. See what creative solutions work for your table. I folded an extra tile over the edges of the tabletop to cover the thickness of the MDF. This will make the mirrored top look more substantial.

Once you are happy with the arrangement of tile sheets, score the surface of the tabletop by scratching it up a little with a craft knife. Then smear a thin layer of PVA across the top, using a piece of card to spread it evenly over the surface.

Carefully place the tiles in position, making sure you fold an extra tile over the edge. Add a lick of glue around the sides of the MDF and press these tiles neatly down. [2]

Now for the peacock feathers. Snip the shaft off each feather, so you have just the feathered 'eye' and a little below it.

Turn the feathers over and skim off the thickness of the shaft with a craft knife – you want them to be as flat as possible, so they'll lie flush against the table leg, rather than looking like they might flutter off. [3]

Spray the feathers with clear craft sealant. This will preserve the fluffiness – if you apply varnish to the feathers without sealing them first, the barbs will separate and just look wet, and you'll have to start again.

When the sealant if completely dry, squirt a little spray mount on the back of the feathers, and press them onto the top of each front table leg. Do this gently, so the barbs remain intact. Press down any bits that pop up, then lick over them with a little paint-on varnish. [4]

TEACH ME A LESSON

wallpapered screen

After years of hanging around in unfashionable circles (geddit?), wallpaper has undergone a renaissance that shows no signs of abating. But for the commitment phobes among us, it's a little too permanent, especially if you think that steam-stripping is a type of spa treatment. What's more, before you even have the chance to decide you hate it, there's all that wrestling to get the stuff stuck on uneven walls in the first place (stepladders and heels, don't get me started). It's enough to make you scream. So try making a screen instead.

A screen offers the same opportunity to make a statement as a wall, with the added bonus of being more flexible. It hides ugly corners and is two-faced – which is great if you can't decide between Cole & Son's 'Woodstock' (see left) and Neisha Crosland's 'Hollywood Grapevine'. A screen is simple to make and, when you decide that the Anaglypta revival really was all in your head, it's easy to change.

YOU WILL NEED

1   4 equal-sized panels of wood – plywood is ideal (I used MDF, but it's a little on the heavy side for this application). Buy your wood from a lumber or hardware store (check that they cut wood first – some don't) and get it cut to exactly to the width of your wallpaper. For height, just over 2 yards usually works well, though take into account what you'll be using yours for.

2   6 steel hinges and screws – get the biggest hinges that the width of your wood can take; your lumber store will be able to advise you on this.

3   Drill and screwdriver

4   Paint – this is for the edges and any panels that you don't want to cover in paper. I used blackboard paint on two panels.

5   Paintbrush, roller and paint tray

6   Wallpaper paste

7   White coloring pencil

METHOD

Paint one side of each panel and all the edges. **[1 and 2]** I used blackboard paint, so that I could write menus café-style when friends came over. (In practice, my husband uses it as a sounding board for his stomach – I've come home to anything from 'feed me!!' to requests for Steak Tartare, Veal Milanese and 'An assortment of dead animals, please'. I'm a vegetarian.)

Next, use the paint roller to apply wallpaper paste to the unpainted side of the panels. Rolling on the paste, rather than brushing it on, gives a flatter, more even distribution.

Place the wallpaper gently over it – here, you'll be glad you had the wood cut to the width of your paper, as there's no fiddly matching up. Gently smooth the paper from the center outwards with your hands or a clean, dry roller. **[3]** Leave to dry.

Next, mark the edge of one of the boards, 7³/4 in. in from the top and bottom. Hold your hinge here and mark the holes with

a coloring pencil. You need to mark for hinges on only one side of the two outside panels and on both sides of the two center panels. Make sure the wallpaper is going in the correct direction.

Drill pilot holes for the hinges – this stops the wood from splitting when you screw them in. It is a good idea to line up the panels on the ground, with the two edges that you intend to hinge together facing up, to double-check the alignment before you start drilling.

Screw in the hinges, making sure that the screws go in straight. **[4]** Attach all the hinges on the correct corresponding sides. Easy.

upholstered drop-in seat

Who says that just because our mums and dads have matching chairs we should, too? Besides, these do match – just in a different kind of way.

The word 'upholstery' conjures up images of Women's Institute meetings and evening classes in draughty strip-lit sixth-form colleges. But, in reality, upholstery is the quickest way to revamp boring old furniture, making it as hip as the new material you choose. While antiques and big projects such as sofas are best left to the professionals, a drop-in seat can be done by a novice in a couple of hours. Encouraging if you have your sights set on six.

Dining chairs can be picked up anywhere from eBay to auction houses; you'll find that sets of four or more command a higher price than the odd ones and twos. Don't be too led by bargain hunting – remember, you'll be living with these pieces – but it is worth considering buying odd chairs of a similar style, as I have here. Stain the wood (or whitewash it if you prefer, LA style) and upholster the seats to match. The result will be a fabulously witty mix of period and repro finds that haven't cost the earth but look like a snazzy designer collection.

Read through all the instructions before you start and assess the condition of your chair; this will help you decide which of the materials listed on the right you will need to upholster your particular chair.

YOU WILL NEED

1 Chair with a drop-in seat (place your hand underneath the chair seat and push; if it pops out, it's a drop-in seat)

2 Hand-held staple gun

3 Upholsterer's tacks (buy a box of 3/8 in. (10mm) and a box of 1/2 in. (13mm)

4 Tack lifter (this has a V-shaped end that prises tacks out)

5 Flat-ended screwdriver (this will do if you don't have a tack lifter)

6 Small hammer (a magnetic one to pick up dropped tacks is useful)

7 Polyester batting (2oz batting is fine for this application; you need a piece 2 in. bigger than the chair seat all round)

8 2 inch-thick foam, the same size as your seat (you only need this if you intend to start from scratch – see the following instructions. If your seat just needs plumping out, buy more filling identical to the filling already in your chair)

9 Webbing (buy the black and white herringbone variety, as this is the strongest sort)

10 Muslin (tough white cotton used to protect the outer fabric from the stuffing; you need a piece 3/4 in. bigger than your chair frame)

11 Burlap (sacking-like cloth that holds the stuffing in place – 10oz burlap is ideal; a piece 1/2 in. longer and wider than your seat)

12 Fabric, 3 in. bigger than your chair frame all round (pick a fabric suitable for upholstery, which will be stronger than normal fabric. Check with your supplier that the fabric you want to use complies with current fire and safety standards. Some fabrics are fire retardant, while others can be used with a fire-retardant barrier cloth. Bear in mind that close-weave fabrics are generally easier to clean than velvets and wider weaves which hold dust and dirt.

13 Web strainer (this is a wooden tool that enables sufficient leverage to pull the webbing taut enough to stop the seat from sagging for several years. If you have a strong wrist, a small piece of hard wood that you can wrap the webbing around will do.

Pop out the seat and flip it upside down. Remove the canvas or burlap from the underside. This will either be tacked or stapled in place, so use your tack lifter or the flat end of a screwdriver as a lever to prise out the staples or tacks. **[1]** If you are using a screwdriver, you may need a bit more force to remove tacks, so gently tap the handle of the screwdriver with a hammer.

Next, take off the fabric cover, using your screwdriver or tack lifter to lever out the staples or tacks that are holding it in place. Keep this on one side to use as a pattern for your new cover.

Underneath this outer fabric, the seat will be covered with batting and possibly muslin –

protective layers to cover the seat's stuffing and stop it from rubbing against the outer fabric. Remove both.

If the seat is in generally good order, you'll only need to plump out the existing stuffing before you recover it – this is likely to be the case with any reasonably modern chair, and it saves you a heck of a lot of work. To check, look underneath the seat. If the webbing (the heavy, often black and white, braid criss-crossing the bottom of the seat frame) isn't sagging or starting to disintegrate, you're in luck, so go on to the next step, headed 'If you just need to plump out the seat'. If the webbing is looking saggy, however, this is a job well worth doing properly,

so go to the step headed 'If the webbing looks bad and you need to replace it'.

If you just need to plump out the seat

The stuffing will be in a couple of layers. Carefully lift the top layer and add two new handfuls of the same sort of padding into the center. **[2]** It's vital that you use similar fillings, as different fillings (such as horse hair and polyester batting) will clump together like dreadlocks, leaving you with a lumpy seat. Go to the section titled 'Attaching batting and the outer fabric' on page 75.

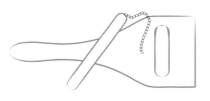 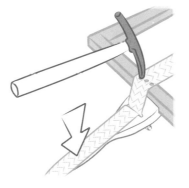 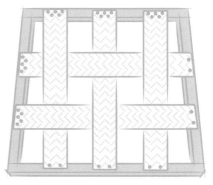

*If the webbing looks bad and
you need to replace it*
Make a note of how many
existing strands of webbing there
are crossing the bottom
of your chair seat – most chairs
have two strands each way, but
wider seat frames, such as early
Victorian styles, will have three
(see above, right). You need to
buy enough webbing to replace
whatever is already there; take a
good look at where it is
positioned, as you'll need to
replace it in the same way.

Remove the existing webbing by
levering out the tacks with a tack
lifter or the flat end of your
screwdriver. You need to replace
webbing evenly, always working
from the back to the front, then
from side to side. If you have an
uneven number of strands, start
in the middle (as I have here).

Without cutting your length of
webbing, fold the end under just
more than $1/4$ in., and place it
fold-down on the back edge of
the chair frame. Tack three $1/2$ in.
(13mm) tacks in a straight line
along the fold and two more a
little further in, so your tacks
look like a dot-to-dot 'W' shape.

Insert the webbing into the
strainer (see above, left) so the
recessed lip is facing upwards
and stretch it tightly to the front
of the frame. Place the strainer
so that the lip hooks onto the
underside of the front of the
seat frame. Hold tightly and
lever down to create tension in
the webbing (see above, center).

Once taut, secure the webbing to
the frame by hammering in three
tacks in a straight line,
as before, approximately 2 in.
apart. Cut the webbing with
$3/4$ in. to spare and fold this
excess over (hiding the line of
three tacks) and hammer in two
more tacks. Your five tacks will
be in the same configuration as
on the other side of the frame,
only three of these tacks will
be under the webbing. Repeat
for the rest of the webbing.

To cover the webbing, before fixing the padding on top, cut a piece of burlap 1/2 in. bigger then your seat frame. Keep the grain of the fabric in line with the strands of webbing running from the front to the back of the chair seat. Fold the burlap over 1/2 in. and, with the fold facing upwards, tack this edge to the back of your seat frame using 3/8 in. (10mm) tacks. **[3]**

Stretch the burlap tightly to the front of the seat frame and temporarily secure it with three tacks – make sure you keep the grain of the fabric straight. It's easy to tell whether you have the grain straight, as the fabric will become tense in a straight line when you pull it, rather than feeling like it's skewing off to one side. Do the same with the sides. Then, working from the middle of each side towards the corners knock in tacks about 1 in. apart.

Fold the raw edges up and over, and tack them down.

Replacing the seat padding with foam
Get a piece of 2 inch-thick foam cut to 1/4 in. bigger than the size of your seat frame and place it centrally on the burlap. **[4]**
The reason the foam needs to be slightly bigger is so that it creates a dome in the center of the seat and the edges curl over, forming a nice curve once they're pulled tightly down.

Attaching batting and the outer fabric

Cut a piece of polyester batting 2 in. bigger all round than the seat frame. You need to make sure that the batting is no bulkier than than the previous covering, since adding thickness that amounts to more than what was previously on the seat could mean that your finished seat won't fit back into the frame – which really would be a pain at this stage. Stretch the batting very tightly over the frame and staple it on the underside, leaving the corners. Trim off the excess along each side. **[5]** Pinch the surplus batting across the corners and chop away the excess, then staple down. **[6]**

Cut your covering fabric 3 in. bigger all round than the seat. You can use the old cover as a pattern, if you prefer.

Spread out the covering fabric right side down on the floor or on a table and place the padded seat, padding side down, on top of it. Making sure the fabric is straight, fold it up to the frame and lightly hammer in one tack on the underside of the seat frame in the center of the back, front and each side. This is to hold the fabric temporarily in place, so don't bang the tacks in all the way.

Once the fabric is positioned, staple the center of the back securely, a $1/4$ in. or so in from the edge of the frame. Then pull the fabric very tight and staple the front, working from the middle out towards the corners, as you did when attaching the burlap.

Staple each side in the same way, leaving the corners as you

did with the batting.

The corners – like the batting – will have lots of excess fabric. Pull the center of this excess taut and, holding it super-tight, staple a few times underneath the seat. Now cut away the excess fabric. Fold one side under, creating a neat vertical pleat (see page 151). Professionals tap this gently with a hammer to get a completely flat finish. The pleat may take a couple of goes, but it's well worth getting it right. Once you've cracked it, staple it firmly in place.

Cut a piece of muslin $1/4$ in. bigger than the seat. Turn the edge under and tack this neatly onto the bottom of the seat, hiding the messy stapling. Now pop your new seat into the frame.

wooden 'Vogue' placemats

You can buy cheap placemats practically anywhere, but mostly they're plastic horrors the size of a ground sheet that bring to mind dining in the Little Chef circa 1985. Check out these cheeky chopping-board mats and you'll see in an instant why you need to make your own. The mats last for ever, don't require any technical skill or sewing and are ideal to make with children (the perfect rainy day project) and what better use for kiddie art? I made these with a friend's teenage daughter, Issi. A real photography fan, she picked her favorite images from a book of vintage *Vogue* covers so, as chic as they look, I can't really take credit for them.

YOU WILL NEED _____

1   A thin plank of pale wood, such as pine or cherry, chopped into pieces, from a lumber store
2   Lazertran 'Waterslide' transfer paper or equivalent product
3   Sandpaper
4   Scissors
5   A toner-based printer or photocopier (most printers and photocopiers are toner-based)
6   Turpentine
7   Matt oil-based varnish
8   Soft paintbrush for applying varnish
9   Soft decorator's brush (3/4 in. is ideal)

METHOD

Go to your local lumber store and buy a plank of wood. You need to ask them to cut the plank you have bought into 12 in. lengths – as I did to the dismay of Rory, who works in my local lumber store and had to cut this cherry-wood plank into 15 pieces (you have to buy a whole plank, I didn't actually want 15 placemats, you understand). Not all lumber stores cut wood, so call and check first. Don't, whatever you do, cut the wood yourself – it'll take for ever and raggy edges are much less likely with professional equipment. Use the sandpaper to smooth away any rough edges.

Decide on a design for each mat. Anything can work here – a photo of every family member for the ultimate personalized place settings, children's drawings, vintage wallpaper or magazine covers.

Print the images you choose onto the chalky side of the transfer paper using a toner-based printer (practically all domestic printers are toner-based). Or go to a copy shop and ask them to print the pictures onto your transfer paper. Make sure that you stipulate which side of the transfer paper to print on.

Let the inks dry thoroughly – this will take about 30 minutes. Then trim your picture to size, cutting off any borders, so you are just left with the picture that you want on your mat.

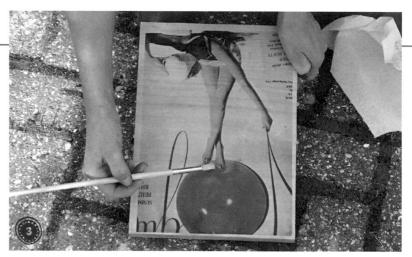

Carefully lower the picture into a washing-up bowl of clean water and leave it for a minute or so. [1]

The transfer will come away from the backing paper in the water. Gently peel away the transfer and discard the backing paper. The transfer is flimsy so be overly cautious to avoid tearing it. [2]

Lay the transfer on a plate to dry. You'll know when it's dry as the background of the picture will turn white. When the transfer is completely dry, brush your receiving surface (the wood) with pure turpentine. Carefully slide the transfer onto the surface.

VERY gently, using feather-like strokes, smooth over the image with your soft brush and a little more turpentine. The image will begin to 'melt' into the surface, so your picture will look like it is printed in the wood. Don't overwork this or force the transfer into the grain – this will happen by itself overnight. [3]

When the image is completely dry, apply three or four coats of oil-based matt varnish, leaving it to dry after each coat. [4]

Voila, personal couture kitchenware.

Hallway

in between places

mirrored stair rises

If you're loving up your living room, beautifying your bedroom and going crazy in the kitchen, what about the spaces in between? Why shouldn't the A to Bs of a home, such as stairs, be treated to a *soupçon* of craftiness, too? I'm not talking pink neon lighting or sheepskin pads on every step – that's way too 1970s, and not in a good way. But a few subtle tiles between steps could be the difference between dreary and delightfully Studio 54.

YOU WILL NEED _____

1   Uncarpeted stairs – one-floor flat dwellers need not apply
2   Mirrored tiles
3   Double-sided tape
4   PVA glue
5   Piece of card or a brush to apply the glue
6   Craft knife
7   Metal ruler
8   Cloth

METHOD

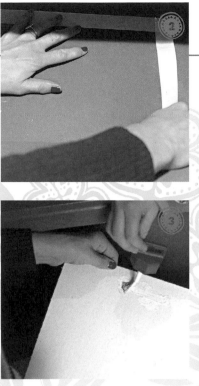

Measure the rise of your stairs. I'm using stairs in a converted warehouse, which have a flat diagonal back, but the rules are same for normal stairs.

Using these measurements, work out how many sheets of tile will fit on your stair rises. Carefully cut the sheets to size using a craft knife. To make cutting easier, bend the sheet along the row of tiles you want to cut to expose the backing. (When the sheets of tiles are flat, the tiles sit flush against one another, making it harder to cut between them.) Don't cut any tiles in half – they'll look like snapped razor blades. If your measurement falls in the center of a tile, round it down to the nearest whole tile. You don't need to completely fill the rise; in fact, even a couple of rows in the center will look great.

Score the area of the rise that you want to cover, by scratching it with a craft knife. Wipe away any dust with a cloth. [1]

Stick a rectangle of double-sided tape around the area of the rise that you intend to tile. [2]

Smear PVA glue across the tile backing. Make sure you spread it right to the edges, using a piece of card or a brush for an even application. [3]

Remove the backing from the double-sided tape and gently lay the tiles in place. [4] Hold them for a few minutes, lightly pressing across the whole surface area so that the glue and tape adhere.

wild-style woven chair seat

Do you have a saggy old chair that's in need of a more pert seat, but no time for the painstaking precision of weaving? Follow the lead of two Brazilian brothers, Humberto and Fernando Campana. These São Paulo-based designers take found items – old bits of rope, garden hose and stuffed toys – and create wonderfully witty pieces of furniture – chairs, tables and stools – using a modern take on a traditional craft practiced in Brazilian *favelas*. My favorite are their Vermelha Chair and Chair Verde. For both of these the brothers tied, wove and knotted an abundance of brilliantly colored cord through a metal frame. They then cast it in resin, which no doubt made it horribly uncomfortable to sit on.

Forget the resin casting – that's a pain in the ass (quite literally) – but do get inspired by their haphazard approach to weaving. The results will add a dash of tongue-in-cheek charm and Latin exuberance to any interior. And, given the arbitrary process, you actually can't go wrong.

YOU WILL NEED

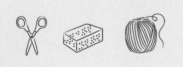

1. A chair frame – whether your chair was originally upholstered, rushed or caned, it can easily be woven using this method
2. Black wood wax and a soft cloth to apply it
3. Brightly colored macramé jute (or string, though this will be a little coarser) and beads. I used about 100 yards of jute and 15 beads.
4. Fine sandpaper and a damp cloth
5. Material for découpage (optional) – see page 42
6. Scissors
7. Lighter

METHOD

To prepare the chair, remove all traces of the old seat covering (reeds, canework, whatever), then sand it lightly and wipe away the dust with a slightly damp cloth. If your chair was originally caned and has lots of little holes in it, it is a good idea to fill them using wood filler. Having said this, most of the frame will be covered, so no one will ever know if you decide to leave it.

Polish the frame before you start work on the seat. If you intend to découpage as I have, do not apply wax to the places on the chair frame where you want to stick pictures, as wax repels water-based adhesives and varnishes, so they'll slip off. I used a traditional black wax, which is a dark gloopy mixture that you rub into the surface with a soft cloth (it's very easy and produces results a little more subtle than a wood stain). It isn't essential to use black, but dark colors will make the bright seat look electric by contrast.

Also, giving the wood a deeper shade makes it look older (as wood darkens with age) – ideal if you are aiming for a traditional Arts and Crafts feel with the frame.

I découpaged a few birds on the back struts of my chair (see page 42). You'll find that bright colored jute on its own on the seat will look very stark. Adding flashes of a similar color elsewhere helps to pull the look together.

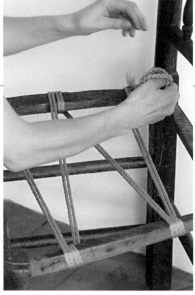

Cut two 10 yard lengths of macramé jute. Fold each piece of jute exactly in half. Starting at one corner, wrap the folded end of one piece around the side of the frame, creating a loop, and pop the two long ends through this loop. Pull the free ends tight, so the loop fits snugly around the frame, securing it to the chair. In macramé-speak, this is called a lark's head (you can casually throw this into conversation to give yourself a professional edge).

Now you have two strands next to each other. Wrap these lengths into a neat bundle or around a piece of card, so they are easier to work with. Keeping the two strands parallel bring them across to the opposite side of the frame, wrap them around once, and then take them back in a diagonal line to the other side. Wrap them around the frame again, and repeat. Make sure you hold the jute tightly and pull it as hard as you can whenever you wrap it around the frame – you need tension to prevent the seat from sagging.

I found that zigzagging from side to side a few times, then going from front to back, interlacing every time I crossed an adjacent strand, made a good foundation. After that, try diagonal lines, too, adding on a new piece of doubled-up jute, as before, whenever you need to. The difference between this freestyle weaving and traditional weaving is you do not need to work front to back, then left to right. There are no rules, except to interlace with any strands that you cross.

When you start to run out of cord, wrap the remaining 9 in. or so around one of the front legs and secure it at the back of the leg using a reef knot. I left the ends dangling and attached beads, then burnt off the raggy ends with a lighter.

If your chair requires use more coverage in the seat, either two or four parallel yarns. Thicker lines in the weave look deliberate, which can be a good thing when you're taking such a haphazard approach (you'll get fewer comments along the lines of: 'Is it supposed to be like that?'). Attach any extra strands of macramé jute either at one side or at the back and continue your wild weaving until it's looking busy enough.

Secure the ends with reef knots on the underside of the chair frame. Or wrap them around the chair legs and knot bright beads onto the dangling ends. Presto, you're done.

macramé hanging basket

Macramé is the art of tying decorative knots and the ultimate 1970s homecraft. It's calming to do and the twiddling processes are sheer yoga for the hands. What better antidote to hours in front of a computer screen? We've seen macramé sneaking into fashion in recent years, mainly in the form of designer bikinis, but now – ignore ridicule – it's a must-have in the home.

Yes, contemporary macramé is deeply now. Gone are tangled string wall-hangings and plant-pot holders (with yards of dusty spider plant cascading down the sides). In are fresh citrus colored jutes, outsize twelve-arm macramé chandeliers, knotty love seats suspended from the ceiling and acid-colored hanging baskets.

An adorable entry-level project, one that you'll actually find a use for, is this bold basket. Bursting with color it'll liven up any space, indoors or out, with a sly wink at knot art's hippy heritage. Macramé looks complex, but don't be put off. For this basket all you need to learn are two different types of knot. Once you have mastered these, you can quickly progress to original works of your own.

So, clear a space, get knotting and head to the garden center – you could do with a new plant. Not only do plants purify the air, they also absorb noise and counteract some of the chemicals that have been linked to Sick Building Syndrome. What's not to like?

YOU WILL NEED

1   90 yards of 1/8 in. synthetic macramé cord (it sounds like a lot but it doesn't go far). You can use different colors but macramé is so knobbly that one bright color looks best, as it keeps the focus on the texture.
2   20 wooden beads (you can get all sorts if you're prepared to look, even parrot-shaped ones)
3   Lighter
4   6 metal hoops, 2 in. diameter (available from macramé suppliers)
5   PVA craft glue (something a little tackier than your usual paper and wood-bonding PVA)
6   Scissors

METHOD

Cover your six 2 in. hoops with macramé cord. To do this, squirt a 1 in. line of glue onto the hoop. Take the end of a length of macramé cord and, leaving the last 3/4 in. free, press it firmly onto the glued section. Holding the glued cord in place, start to wind the cord tightly around the hoop, from the center of the glued section out. Continue until you get to the other side, leaving no gaps. Tie the two ends together, then singe the knot with a lighter, so that the fibers melt together; this way the knot won't come undone.

Now, snip a separate length of cord, about half a yard long, and set it aside. Cut the remaining cord into eight pieces of equal lengths and fold each piece in half. Take one of your covered hoops and attach the eight

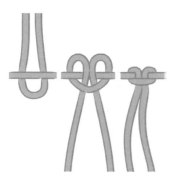

pieces of cord using a lark's head (see below), and pull tight.

Hang the hoop from a door knob, as this will make it easier to work with. You will have sixteen strands hanging from the hoop. Divide the strands into four (each section will have four strands). Keeping the strands in their sections, measure a yard from the hoop and wrap the rest of the section into a bundle. This will stop the lengths getting tangled when you start knotting.

You now have four sections to work with. Following the photographs below, start by

tying a half knot, which is really just a slip knot. **[1 and 2]** Treat each four-cord section as one strand (in the photographs I've used one cord to represent each section to keep it clear).

Hold the central two strands taut. Take the left-hand strand over the central two and under the right-hand strand. Take the right-hand strand under the central strands and up over the left-hand strand.

Tie eight half knots. This creates the main stem at the top of the plant holder. Your grip on the cords should be firm, but don't

a   b

yank them; try to keep the tension the same throughout.

You will find that continuously tying half knots creates an interesting spiral. Rather than following this awkwardly with your hands, turn the hoop to keep your knots at the front.

Now undo one of the four-cord bundles. Bundle up the end of each cord, leaving a yard to work with as before.

Tie fifteen half knots (as you did before, but this time it'll be thinner, as you're using four rather than sixteen cords). You'll find that the two 'working cords' – that is, the outside ones you're tying with – are getting shorter, so you need to swap them over.

To do this, add a bead in. Take the two working cords and, using a lighter, singe and pinch the ends. [5 and 6] Then thread the cord through the center of a bead and pull it up to where the fifteen half knots that you've tied finish. [3] Taking the other two cords (the supporting or 'core' cords), tie twelve half knots under the bead. [4]

Take the section of four cords directly opposite the section that you've just worked on and repeat the above steps.

You should have two sections remaining. Take one and undo the bundled-up cords. You will have four strands hanging down. Bundle up the end of each strand, leaving a yard of each

cord to work with. You're now going to do a square knot, which is like the half knot, but from alternate sides so that it doesn't spiral round.

To create a square knot tie one knot exactly the same as the half knots you've already tied (see above, **a**). Then, starting from the other side, reverse the knot (see above, **b**). Pull the cords taut before you tie the next knot (see above right, **c** and **d**).

Continue alternating in this way, until you have tied fifteen knots.

After fifteen knots, swap the central and outer cords by adding on a bead, as you did before. Tie twelve more square knots below the bead. Repeat

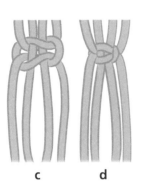

c   d

this with the remaining section of four cords. All your knots should finish at the same place. If they do not, you have used differing tensions. This is no big deal, just hold the core cords taut and ease the working cords down or up until they match.

Measure 7 in. down your cord. After this gap, tie two square knots. Do the same with all four sections.

Now, rather than keeping each section together, take two right-hand cords from one section and two left-hand cords from the section directly next to it. Measure 4 in. down from the last knots you tied. After the 4 in. gap tie two square knots.

Pulling the cords together from different sections like this will create a deep 'V' shape.

Now take another of the hoops that you covered earlier and loop the middle two cords around it.

Tie a knot underneath to secure your hanging to the hoop. Then tie twenty more knots under-neath it. Repeat the above for each section, so the hoop is attached horizontally in the center of your hanging (fit for a plant pot to rest on). As with the top sections, I alternated the knots I used; two opposing sections were done in square knots, the other two using half knots. Feel free to add beads in too, wherever you fancy.

Gather the ends of the cords from your plant-pot holder and, starting directly below the last knots, wrap the 19$\frac{1}{2}$ in. cord you cut earlier round the hanging cords to keep them together. Keep 5–6 in. at the start of the wrapping cord free. Wind this together with the rest of the cords. Once you've tightly wrapped 4 in. or so tie the two ends together and singe the knot. Now you'll have a 'ponytail' effect with lots of free ends hanging down. Trim these down a little so they don't look scraggy – varying lengths tend to look best.

Place a bowl in the holder, resting it on the horizontal hoop. Tie the other hoops to the free ends or attach a bead to each of the free ends, as I have. Again, singe the knot underneath to prevent if from unravelling.

Now for that macramé chandelier and love-seat …

Living room

boutique craft for luxury lounging

vintage scarf cushions

Sumptuous new cushions update a room instantly and are a great way to add a flash of color or pattern. Make them yourself and you have the perfect use for those old scarves that you haven't looked at in years.

Vintage-scarf cushions – using designer scarves if possible – are an easy way to landing a seriously chic designer punch in your living room. When choosing scarves to make your cushion covers from, don't be afraid of mismatching fabrics, just keep an eye out for patterns that sit well together, and an open mind about color schemes. You'll be limited by whatever materials you have, but bear in mind that unexpected combinations often look fabulously fresh. Oh, and by the way, according to 1970s' Women's Institute books, making a cushion is 'well within the scope of the average needlewoman'. So there you are.

YOU WILL NEED

1 2 same-sized silk scarves that match or clash well (mine were 28^1/$_4$ in. square; if you cannot find two scarves that match, cut a square of fabric the same size as the scarf you want to use and sew a zigzag stitch around the perimeter to prevent it from fraying)

2 Lightweight Vilene interfacing to back both scarves (this is a thin, fusible material that makes delicate cloth more durable)

3 Pins

4 Needle

5 Sewing machine, if you have one

6 Matching thread

7 Matching plastic zipper, 4 in. shorter than the edge of the cushion

8 Cushion pad (down filling is nicest, unless you're allergic to feathers). This should be the same size as your scarves, even though the seam allowance will render the cover slightly smaller when finished. As with the cushion on page 26, making the cover a tad smaller than the cushion is what makes the finished thing look puffy.

9 Colored pencil or tailor's chalk

10 Scissors

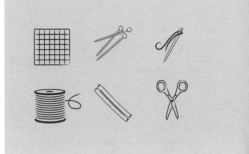

Cut a piece of Vilene the same size as each scarf and iron to the wrong side of each scarf, using a LOW temperature. [1] Remember, your scarves are silk and you don't want to burn them with a cotton setting. When you are ironing, rather than gliding the iron across the fabric, as you would usually, just gently press it down on a section, then lift and press it on the next bit. Silk tends to move around a lot, so this method will prevent the shape from skewing from a square to a diamond.

Place the right sides of the scarves together. The Vilene will be showing on the outside. You'll be glad you used Vilene, as your vintage prints won't slip around here. Pin together about 2 in. of one side of the cushion cover from both corners, 1½ in. in from the edge of the fabric. This will be the back seam of the cushion cover into which you will insert your zipper. [2]

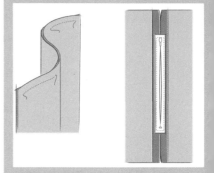

To insert your zipper into this seam, sew 2 in. of the back seam of the cushion cover from each corner, removing the pins as you go. As you've only sewn 2 in. at each end of this seam, you'll be left with a big hole in center of the back seam, which is where the zipper will go.

Open the material out in front of you, with the wrong side facing up. Iron the two 2 in. seams open, and press back the seam allowance on either side of the hole. Flip the fabric over to the right side and pin your zipper into the hole, ensuring the ironed edges meet at the center when the zipper is closed.

Undo the zipper and sew all the way around it, removing pins as you go. Sew as near to the zipper teeth as you can and you'll get a neater finish. If you are using a sewing machine, use the zipper foot, as this will enable you to get as close to the teeth of the zipper as possible.

Now the zipper is in place, the rest is a doddle. Turn the material wrong side out and pin then sew around the remaining three sides, $1/2$ in. in from the edge. You can draw a line with a colored pencil or chalk for a guide, which is a good idea if you're sewing by hand. Sew a few extra stitches at the start and end of your seams to secure them and, if you're hand-sewing, tie a knot in your thread as well.

Snip away the excess fabric diagonally at each corner and iron all your seams open. [3] This makes the cushion neat on the outside. If you don't do this, you'll find that the seams will dip inwards instead of lying flat.

Turn the cushion right side out (by pulling it through the zipper hole), then squash your cushion pad through the hole. Hold the pad tight so that it doesn't stretch the seams (the pad is bigger than the cover, remember).

Now you know what you're doing, zip it up, pat yourself on the back, and work out how many more you need, bearing in mind everyone and the cat will want to claim one for their own.

tapestry cube

With such an amazing pedigree, tapestry has earned its place in this book. Examples exist as far back as the fourth century – a testament to its durability. You can see them, alongside many others, in The Textile Museum, Washington DC. I also recommend checking out the fifteenth-century War of Troy Tapestries in the V&A, London. Incidentally, in case you're wondering why I haven't mentioned the famous Bayeaux Tapestry, which commemorates the Battle of Hastings in 1066, it's because it isn't a tapestry: it's actually embroidery.

The advent of mass-produced fabric during the Industrial Revolution meant that hand-decorating became prohibitively expensive and tapestry all but died, save a few faithful circles where it was nurtured as a recreational pastime. The Arts and Crafts era of the late 1800s allowed tapestry a brief renaissance, encouraged by William Morris, who championed the hand-crafted over the manufactured and was particularly keen on tapestry; for a while it became as coveted as high art. Tapestry hit style radars again – for a less glamorous stint – in the 1970s, alongside hippy pastimes such as bean art. Now it's been out of fashion for so long that it's well due a revival.

Let's have a go at bringing back that faded glory with a new spin. Mixing old techniques with new is the height of fashion, and the making is easy and fun. This modern cube shakes off needlepoint's old-maid image by combining art with handy extra seating. Once you've mastered the technique (one simple stitch), it is not difficult to make contemporary designs that'll last a lifetime and have future generations gawping in admiration. Get stuck in, and you won't regret it. It's a first-class ticket to your very own family heirloom.

YOU WILL NEED

For the tapestry

1 Tapestry canvas, 16$\frac{1}{2}$ x 16$\frac{1}{2}$ in. (there are lots of different types, in a variety of mesh sizes; 10 and 12 count are most popular – the word 'count' refers to the number of stitches you'll get per inch. This swan was stitched on 7 count rug canvas, which is a very low count and requires very thick yarn. If you like the overblown look of these outsize stitches, try the same; 10 or 12 count will give a more traditional look.)

2 Tapestry wools in a variety of colors (ask your supplier to advise on yarn thicknesses for the canvas you've chosen)

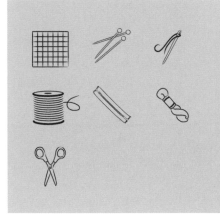

3 Picture or design that you'd like to make into a tapestry (alternatively, you can buy a kit with an image printed on the canvas, which you just stitch over)

4 Piece of graph paper and coloring pencils, or Lazertran Textile transfer paper (or equivalent product)

5 Tapestry needle (this is just a large, blunt needle with a big eye to fit the woolly yarns through)

6 Scissors

For the cube

7 Five squares of fabric the same size as your tapestry (I used an Osborne & Little fabric, an old denim skirt which I cut up, and patches of velvet)

8 Zipper, 10 in. long

9 2 yards bias binding to match your tapestry

10 Sewing machine or needle, thread and dressmaker's pins

11 Filling – polystyrene beads (which can be bought at markets or online), or old clothes or tights (which will give a firmer shape)

METHOD

To create a tapestry using your own design or picture, you need to transfer the image onto your canvas or create a counted thread pattern on graph paper. Both methods are very simple.

Either, print your image to scale, in color, onto transfer paper (Lazertran Textile is ideal), then iron the transfer onto the canvas and peel off the backing paper. You can then use the colors transferred onto the canvas as a guide for where to stitch and which colors to use.

Or, to create a pattern, mark ¼ in. in on each side of your canvas and count how many vertical threads there are in the 15¾ in. between these two points. Cut a square piece of graph paper, with the same number of squares as you just counted – each square represents a stitch. You can print graph paper from freepatternsonline.com (this gem of a site is packed with designs, advice and blank graphs). Photocopy the paper so it's the same size as your finished tapestry will be. Print the image you want to use to scale and

hold it up against a window. Place the graph paper on top, so you can see the design through it. Color in each square, as per the design underneath. As each square needs to be just one color, this will simplify and pixilate the picture a little.

That's the hard bit over. The stitching is easy and wonderfully calming. You can do it anywhere, so keep it in your handbag for boring bus rides, or block off an

afternoon, get a friend round and stitch in between cream scones. There's just one stitch to learn – the tent stitch. It's small, diagonal and the most commonly used stitch in needlepoint.

Thread your tapestry needle and pull the yarn through the canvas from back to front, leaving a ½ in. of yarn at the back (you'll stitch over this in your first few stitches to secure it – a knot could pop through the holes).

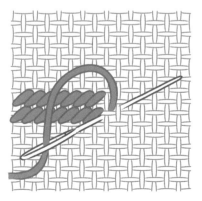

Working from right to left, thread your needle back through the nearest diagonal hole, above and to the right of where you started. There! Your first stitch. Continue in this way, creating lots of forward-sloping stitches, until you've finished a row (see diagram below, left).

Take the yarn on the underside of the canvas to the row of holes beneath your first row of stitches. You'll now be working in the other direction, from left to right. Bring your needle up and stitch diagonally right, so the top of this stitch goes through a hole shared by the bottom of a stitch in the row above (see diagram below, right).

Continue in this way, so that all your stitches slope in the same direction. Rather than working a full row at a time, work in patches of color, using either your transferred print on the canvas or the graph paper pattern to guide you as to which color to use where. Continue until your tapestry is complete.

To make the cube
Sew zigzag stitch around the five squares to prevent fraying.

Sew your zipper into the center of the seam between two squares of fabric (see pages 96–97). Use the most robust fabric – I sewed my zipper between a piece of denim and a thick upholstery fabric.

Keeping the right side of each piece on the same side, sew a third square onto one of the first two (opposite the zipper); then sew a fourth square to the other end of that, to create a long strip. [1] Then sew the two ends of the strip together, with right sides facing, so you have a cube shape, minus the top and bottom.

Enclose the edges of the tapestry in bias binding and sew it on. Then pin the tapestry onto one open end of your 'cube', making sure that when you turn it right side out the tapestry will be on the outside and all the raggy edges will be on the inside.

Keeping the cube inside out, undo the zipper, then pin on the final square, and sew.

Diagonally snip off the excess fabric at each corner, then pull the cube right side out and fill it with stuffing. If you're using polystyrene beads make a funnel from card or paper. [2] When the cube is full and as firm as you want, close the zipper.

fabric découpage standard lamp and table

A little recklessness with dull old furniture can really pay off. With fabric découpage you can create quirky pieces from the most boring stuff and it won't cost a penny. The idea of covering objects with fabric was last big in the 1970s. *House & Garden* annuals from the era are packed with whole rooms, including four-poster beds, chests and chairs, covered from top to toe in psychedelic prints so bright that the owners probably never needed to take acid.

Now the idea is back and canny designers are selling quirky one-offs for small fortunes. But you needn't buy, provided you have some old furniture to hand: it's easy and you can make pieces that suit your taste perfectly – much more stylish and savvy than buying an overpriced oddity that you'll need to decorate your sitting room around.

For a modern look, and to make matching the pattern easier, spotty fabrics are a good bet. Think of the abstract artist Bridget Riley, famous for her optical 1960s output, and get busy with the glue.

YOU WILL NEED _____

For the lamp stand

1   Standard lamp (look for a shape you find appealing, as this will be highlighted by its new covering)
2   Fabric (go for a simple pattern, preferably with a plain colored background, such as spots, as these are easier to match than larger repeats. Cottons, like the one I have used here, are very cheap.)
3   Sandpaper
4   Clear sealant (available at hardware stores – Plasti-kote is a good one)
5   PVA
6   Jar (for mixing up the glue solution)
7   Paintbrush (1/4 in. wide)

For the lampshade

8   Old lampshade frame
9   Fabric (either to match or coordinate with the fabric you've used on your lamp stand)
10 Adhesive card, such as Laminex (available from craft stores)
11 Bias binding to match your fabric (sufficient to go around the top and bottom edges of your lampshade)
12 Adhesive fabric tape (you need this only if you have an old bare metal frame – this is unlikely, though, as most lampshade frames are covered in white plastic these days)

13 Tape measure
14 Pencil, ruler and set square
15 Clothes pegs
16 Piece of string
17 Large piece of graph paper
18 Glue gun and glue sticks
19 Scissors

Lightly sand your lamp stand, to get a rough surface for the glue to stick to. The fabric will all peel off if you don't bother.

Spread your fabric out on the ground, outside, and spray it on both sides with a clear sealant. [1] This stops it from stretching and going wrinkly when you stick it down.

You need to cut the fabric into little pieces. However, do this as you go along – once you get the knack, you'll have an idea of the size and shape you'll need for different types of surfaces. If

you're covering a curved surface such as this standard lamp, start off by cutting a few pieces 1/2 in. wide by 2 in. long. If the surface is mainly flat, you can use bigger pieces – as you'll see once you get sticking.

Mix the PVA with a little water in a jar (70% PVA to 30% water is about right). Using the paintbrush, paint a patch on the surface of the lamp base to attach your piece of fabric. [2]

Gently smooth your fabric piece onto the gluey surface. [3] Then hold it firmly in place for a few seconds. [4] If the edges peel up, just add a little glue under the edges and press it firmly to the surface. You can also paint

down unruly edges, applying the glue mixture using a brush, on top (it dries clear).

Line up the dots and stick the next piece of fabric down. Continue in this way. [5] Don't worry too much if the dots don't completely match up – it's easy to color in odd halves with a permanent marker pen afterwards.

When you get to tighter curves, cut smaller pieces of fabric to compensate. Another way to get around curves is to cut slits in your patches of fabric (which work like darts in clothing). Overlap the fabric slightly where you have cut it to fit snugly around curves.

old lampshade stripped down for this part.

If the frame you're using is metal, cover it completely by winding adhesive fabric tape first around the rings, then the struts, making sure that there are no gaps. It's unlikely you'll have to do this, however, as most frames are covered in white plastic these days.

NB: It's worth noting that painting patches of solid color to match your fabric is a good way to 'cheat' awkward areas. Don't hesitate to use this easy option with curves, spindles and anything that feels like hard work – it looks just as good.

For a neat finish at the bottom, tuck the fabric under the base of the lamp. (For chair legs and similar pieces that are likely to get moved around, finish in line with the end of the chair leg.)

Once your lamp is completely covered, check for rogue edges that have popped up. Glue them down by applying a little PVA that has not been watered down to the underside, and pressing

the fabric firmly or squeezing it gently with your hand. Allow the glue to dry, then paint a few layers of the PVA solution over the top, leaving it to dry completely between each layer. This will protect and seal your piece, making it durable enough to withstand everyday wear and tear. Five coats is plenty.

The lampshade
You could buy a lampshade that coordinates, but for full impact you should make one in the same fabric. The point of this is to have the whole silhouette in an eyebrow-raising pattern that you would normally associate with, say, clothing and not interior décor. You'll need an

The simplest and most modern shape is a drum lampshade. This is a cylindrical shade that is the same width at the top as it is at the bottom. If this is your first stab at lampshade-making, this is definitely the shape you should go for. Drum shades look particularly good with a straight stem (as this echoes the shape of the shade). A shaped lamp base will probably look better with a coolie shade. This is narrower at the top than the bottom. For either you should make a pattern first.

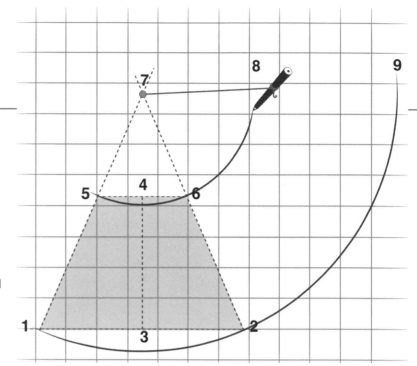

To make the pattern

For a drum lampshade:
Measure the circumference of your lampshade and add $1/2$ in. for an overlap. Draw a rectangle on your graph paper, this width, by the height you want finished shade to be. Use a set square and the grid lines on your paper to get perfect right angles.

Cut this out, then attach it to your lampshade frame with clothes pegs to check it fits properly. It should be an exact fit, with a $1/2$ in. overlap. If it is not, trim the pattern down or add slivers until it is. Then go to 'For both shades' on page 122.

For a coolie lampshade:
This is trickier, so make the one above if possible. On graph paper draw a line equal to the diameter of the bottom of your lampshade (1–2 on the diagram, above).

Draw a perpendicular line going upwards from the center of 1–2, equal to the height of your shade (3–4 on the diagram).

Using 4 as the middle, draw a line the same distance as the diameter of the top of your lampshade (5–6 on the diagram).

Draw a line between 1 and 5, and another line between 2 and 6; continue these lines going up your graph paper until they cross (point 7 on the diagram).

Measure the distance between 7 and 5. Anchor a piece of string to point 7 and tie it to your pencil. Draw an arc equal to the circumference of the top of your lampshade, making sure that any point on the line will be exactly the same distance as 7–5. Add $1/2$ in. for the overlap and mark this end point number 8.

Measure the distance between 7 and 1. Change the length of your piece of string to suit this measurement and draw an arc the same distance as the circumference of the bottom of your lampshade. Add $1/2$ in. for an overlap and mark this finishing point as 9.

Cut out the pattern and, using clothes pegs, attach it to your lampshade frame and check that it's an accurate fit. If it is not, trim the pattern down or add slivers until it is. Then go to 'For both shades' on page 122.

For both shades
Once your pattern fits perfectly, cut out the same shape in adhesive card.

Lay your fabric on top of the adhesive card (on the bias if you're making a coolie shade and straight grain if you're making a drum shade). Smooth the fabric with your hands, so there are no wrinkles. Trim the fabric down to the same size as the card, leaving $1/2$ in. overlap at one end. **[1]** Fold this around around the edge of the card and glue down.

Using a glue gun, attach the top of your lampshade to the top ring of the frame first, then move on to the bottom. You'll need to work quickly, so that the glue is still wet when you press the shade onto the frame. Hold each section in place with clothes pegs while it dries. **[2]**

Put a thin line of glue along the overlap and press to secure. Using PVA or double-sided sticky tape, sandwich some bias binding around the top and bottom edges of your lampshade for a neat finish. **[3]**

You're done. Now, what about revamping a coffee table to match? I covered a scuffed 1960s glass-topped table (see page 106). My husband had smashed the glass, hence the sassy mirror top.

crazy patchwork ottoman

Crazy patchwork is one of the simplest forms of patchwork. It requires no planning and very little skill, making it the perfect craft for anyone who doesn't have enough patience for traditional patchwork. The idea is to sew arbitrary scraps of fabric onto a foundation cloth, then hand-embroider or machine-stitch around them to finish. The top-sewing creates its own web-like pattern that unifies the mismatching fabrics.

While it sounds like something that might have come out of the rave era, crazy patchwork was a recycling favorite of settlers in seventeenth-century America. As bed linen and clothing wore out, any parts of the cloth that weren't threadbare were salvaged and sewn to other pieces to create new lengths for bedding or garments. It became popular in England in the middle of the nineteenth century, and from the 1880s it was elevated from its 'make do and mend' roots to luxurious, high-fashion Victorian pastime. Imported silks, exotic prints and sumptuous velvets were sewn over with feather stitches, whipped stems and lazy daisies, as ladies embroidered – quite competitively – to create the most arresting pieces. It's well worth having a look at some of these high-end examples before you start; log on to www.embroiderersguild.com for inspiration.

YOU WILL NEED _____

1   Medium-weight fusible Vilene (enough to cover the area you want to patchwork; this is available from a fabric store)
2   Scraps of fabric of different colors and designs (swatches are perfect for this application. I mixed Liberty and Osborne & Little upholstery fabric with hand-woven Thai silk that I'd bought on holiday, and an old dressing gown)
3   Sewing machine
4   Thread (pick a color that will stand out from your fabrics to create a pattern)
5   Newspaper and pen (to make the pattern)
6   Elastic, sufficient to go around the ottoman, and a safety pin
7   Scissors

METHOD

Don't plan a design – the whole point of crazy patchwork is its random nature – but bear in mind that a predominant color, or a balance of light and dark, will look better than if you chuck literally anything together. **[1]** Make whatever you like – a bedspread, a cushion cover, or a ottoman cover, as I have here.

Cut the background fabric to the size you require. For this ottoman cover, I drew around the hexagon-shaped top on a sheet of newspaper and then cut out this shape in Vilene, adding $^1/_4$ in. all round for the seam allowance. I then made up a long strip of Vilene to the measure-ment of the circumference of the ottoman, plus a $^1/_4$ in. seam allowance at both ends and an extra $1^1/_2$ in. in depth ($1^1/_4$ in. for creating the channel to thread elastic through on the bottom edge and a $^1/_4$ in. seam allowance on the top edge).

Lay the first few patches of fabric, right side up, on the shiny side of the Vilene. This shiny layer is glue that melts when heated by an iron, fusing the fabric to the Vilene. Traditionally patch-

workers sew scraps to something like an old sheet, but using Vilene saves time and pinning and keeps the fabrics from moving about when you're stitching. Starting in one corner and work-ing outwards, arrange your patches as you like and overlap the edges slightly. Using the hottest temperature your patches can withstand, iron them in place by pressing down on each section for about thirty seconds (or until the fabrics have stuck), then lift the iron and go onto the next section. Don't let the iron come into direct contact with the Vilene – it'll stick and it's a nightmare to get off. Con-tinue adding patches until the shape is covered, interspersing a bold color or pattern here and there.

Thread your sewing machine and, using a wide zigzag stitch, sew along all the raw edges. The

idea is to completely enclose the edges within the width of the zigzag. **[2]** To avoid threads pop-ping out and to get clear, definite lines, sew over every line twice (do the whole lot once, then go over it again). If you see yourself as a Victorian lady of leisure, buy fancy threads and give hand-embroidery a go (www.embroiderersguild.com has an index of stitches).

Now sew up the pieces of the ottoman cover. With right sides together, stitch the strip for the perimeter into a continuousring. Pin and sew the top piece on.

Fold the bottom few $^1/_2$ in. under and stitch it down to form a channel. Thread elastic through the channel and stitch the ends together. The cover should grip the bottom of the pouffe snugly to prevent it from slipping off.

photo treatments

Digital photography has brought an end to the mysterious process of creating a photo – leaving your film with white-coated people who'd return an envelope of prints days later that'd have you murmuring, 'Who's he?' and 'Did I really look that bad?'. Now we're in charge. We can see pictures immediately, share them instantly, print selectively and manipulate them in any way we want. We're the authors of our pictorial storytelling and, frankly, don't want to see red eye or greasy 'T' zones ever again.

Using these images to personalize our environment is a natural extension of this ownership and a much more compelling proposition than IKEA prints or books full of yellowing snaps.

The key to creating great photo art is knowing that there are some techniques that you can do in a lo-fi *Blue Peter* kind of way and others that are best left to the professionals (in this case, assume the role of art director). Start by building confidence in your pictures – print off a stack of photographs that you like. If you're worried about your choices get a second opinion; jobs like this are much easier and more fun with a friend on board, preferably one who'll tell you if you look hot or not in pictures.

Then get into the groove of thinking 'Why not?' to having a picture of your own holiday/husband/horse on the wall, if you've taken one that's good enough. After all, your pictures will mean more than someone else's picture will.

Silver backing

Silver backing adds luminescence, accentuates color and reflects light; it'll basically make any image look more zingy.

If you want a modern unframed finish, get this done professionally. If you intend to frame the image, and the picture will not be compromised by being of a lower resolution, you can do this yourself. Photocopy or print your picture onto acetate. Buy a piece of Perspex and silver card the same size. Squirt a LIGHT veil of spray mount onto the silver card and press your acetate image over the top, then frame (see opposite). I created a black and

white picture of my husband pulling my skirt up, using the DIY method **[2]**, while Learn to Dream, a top-end company that specializes in photo art, created a professional color plate of my brother's attempt at elastic flight. **[1]**

Montage picture

DIY collages belong in the bin with clip frames. Nobody is interested in every last detail of your trip to Magaluf, not even you. Modern, well-spaced montages, however, are a different matter. Get a piece of 8x10 paper and select some photos (from a period in your life or a specific event) that look good together, or that actually look better when grouped and telling a story than on their own.

Ask a professional to rejig the composition and blow the whole thing up to a bigger, more impressive size. Nothing is more boring than photo-sized photos. I used images from my own wedding, my brother's wedding and my parents' for a three-weddings-no-funeral montage. Learn to Dream sorted them into a snappy composition

and added in some colored squares. Perfect. I didn't even get my hands dirty. **[1]**

Matching frames

Grouping together framed pictures can be really effective. Just buy a load of old frames in varying styles from charity shops and car boot sales, and spray-paint them to match. Bright colors tend to look awful, so let your pictures do the talking and opt for simple matt white or glossy black. **[2]**

Rejuvenate an old picture

The horse and cart photograph **[1]** is my parents' favorite wedding picture. The photo is faded, damaged and forty years old. The process of rejuvenating an old photo is definitely one to be tackled by a professional, unless you're an absolute whiz on Photoshop and have your own darkroom. In which case, you're probably a photographer already. By meticulously retouching the damaged areas Learn to Dream reproduced the photo as if it had been taken yesterday – albeit with a few dodgy hairdos.

With old pictures the media you choose is critical. I went for photographic paper, which tends to work best for old prints (a zippy new material sometimes looks like it's working against the image).

On a final note, don't go overboard. A couple in each room is plenty. Any more and you will look a little self-obsessed. Especially when you go large-scale like this. If you can't help yourself, put pictures out on rotation – like your summer and winter wardrobes.

scrapbook

A while ago I came across a year-old receipt for a bottle of champagne in the darkest recesses of my wallet. A friend and I had both signed the back underneath a scrawled drunken rant about celebrating my decision to write a book. At the time, I hasten to add, I had no book deal or, for that matter, subject.

The receipt made me think that if I'd stuck it in a photo album along with a picture of us and a trajectory of our limited successes since, well, it would have been funny – and somehow rather poignant. Adding these keepsakes to your photos creates a narrative and one far more evocative than prints alone.

In the seventeenth century, before photography, scrapbooks were hugely popular. People kept albums of 'sayings and observations' and by the eighteenth century they were adding news clippings, paintings, prose and even locks of hair. These tomes were compiled by young ladies of social standing and given pride of place in family drawing rooms.

Since its glamorous heyday scrapbooking has snapped a heel: now the word conjures up images of teenage diaries and pre-schoolers' butterfly paintings. But this doesn't mean you shouldn't scrapbook as the sophisticated Georgians did. Scrapbooking, after all, is as stylish as you make it.

Everyone has a drawer full of mementos: old birthday cards, maps, photos, 'I love NY' stickers, items that recall people or places. These pages look at these little things – the flotsam of the collecting world.

Start by deciding on an event you want to document: a holiday, a friend's hen weekend (the book could be a gift) or the first few gigs of a new band you like – your life as their groupie, perhaps. Then prepare yourself. Take a notebook, jot down experiences and collect as much as you can as you go along – pictures, maps, flyers, flowers, train tickets, recipes.

I put together a few pages of snaps and mementos from a holiday in Majorca. I pinched a recipe for olive tapenade, pressed a few flowers that lined the ancient walks zigzagging the island and collected receipts from the flashy hotel that financially eviscerated us on our last night. A holiday is, after all, much more than the sum of photos in front of tourist attractions.

There aren't any hard and fast rules to scrapbooking; as everyone's experiences are different, so the components of each book will vary. But these guidelines will help enormously, not to mention giving all that junk in a drawer relevance and coherence – and letting it tell the story you kept it for.

- Similar backgrounds will help to hold one event or story together. Here I used walking maps and stitched the routes we'd taken with my sewing machine. Single colors work equally well, as do enlarged photos: a shot of the open road for a road trip across America, a series of graffiti pictures for a mini-break in New York, details of lace for a trip to Malta, or a deserted beach in Sri Lanka. Whatever evokes your experience.

- Use the center of your layout for a few photos. Don't go overboard – often less is more.

- Like pictures on a wall, framing adds to the composition. Frame entire pages by dotting your mementos around them, or perhaps a simple line of sand with a little glue around the edge.

- Add details – pressed leaves, sketches, and notes of things that happened. This DIY approach adds lo-fi simplicity and intrigue to the flat modernity of photography and it's this that will make your scrapbook.

- Most importantly, have fun. Scrapbooks make wonderful mementos and creating them is something children love doing too. The end results are a fascinating glimpse of their perspective on events, as well as something to treasure for ever.

Bedroom

your dream space

scented pouches

Considering estate agents and 'house doctors' say that the smell of coffee or just-baked bread can sell a house, it's surprising that we don't take more note of how evocative scent is. Or perhaps we do, but lazily resort to grim synthetic plug-ins that promise 'Alpine air' but in reality offer something like 'freshly cleaned lavatory'.

In fact, 'olfactory decorating' – 'dressing' a room with scent – has a long and interesting history. The canny deodorant-free Tudors, for instance, would strew their floors with camomile and lavender, which, when crushed underfoot, disguised the smell of body odor, and the Victorians created all sorts of potpourri.

Nowadays, of course, modern technology has given us deodorant. So it's no longer necessary, or desirable, to dump half of your back garden on the bedroom floor. But, with the right herbs and scents, you can create moods in different rooms and keep linen cupboards and wardrobes smelling of roses – or of anything else that takes your fancy.

Pouches are perfect for mood-mapping your home using scent – just pack them with petal, bloom and herb combinations to suit the setting. They're neat, portable and, when made in chic fabrics, make very sweet gifts, especially if you personalize the contents. Try rose and sandalwood for a broken heart, basil for anxiety, or lime and rosemary to inspire and help concentration – a necessity for anyone working from home. Though you might want to reassure the recipients of your hand crafted scented pouches that you're most certainly not dropping Tudor hints about their personal hygiene.

YOU WILL NEED _____

1 Fabric
2 Ribbon
3 Needle and thread
4 PVA glue
5 Coat hanger with plastic arms that you can snap off
6 Herbs / petals / smelly things (It's worth looking into this properly, so you can conjure up a few mood-specific scents of your own. Pop into Neal's Yard for inspiration and take note of anything that you are drawn to – there's often a reason. In the same way that you crave a specific food when your body needs it, you might find that you're drawn to camomile because you're stressed out, or lemon because you're feeling fuggy. I've given some ideas below to get you started.)

Cedar shavings – to get rid of moths

Lavender – a great sleep inducer; also, along with mint, it repels fleas

Bay leaves – apparently they will 'bring the angels of the future closer': that is, they will help you to move forward and see clearly

Rosemary – good for clearing the head and remembrance

Birch – often used in saunas and to alleviate physical ailments

Peppermint – soothes indigestion

Cinnamon sticks – warm spices like cinnamon not only make you think of Christmas, but apparently stop you feeling fluey

Citronella – an insect repellent (pack a pouch to take on holiday)

Coriander – relieves fatigue

Lemon – helps you visualize and purifies the mind; order in bulk if you work at home

Ginger – helps alleviate travel sickness

Marjoram – assists us when we become obsessive; bunny boilers look no further

Camomile – a sleep inducer

You can put your herbs and spices in a plastic bag overnight with essential oils to intensify the scents, so they'll last longer. I tend not to bother, as I like changing them with my moods.

NOTE:
Some people are sensitive to oils and scents – hay fever sufferers might be affected by floral blends, for example – so check first to make sure. Also, if you don't like a smell, there's probably a reason for it. Choose something else.

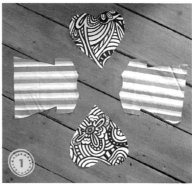

Cut out two pieces of fabric the same shape. By folding your fabric in half and cutting half the shape through both thicknesses, you'll get a more even shape. I went for a heart – which is simple and makes a great-looking gift – and a mini-dress – little versions of clothes like this look really cute hanging in the wardrobe. [1]

For the heart
Lay one of your fabric heart shapes on a flat surface, right side up. Take two pieces of ribbon and pin one end of each to the dip in the top of the heart. Make sure that the rest of the ribbon length is well away from where you are going to sew by pinning it to the center of the heart.

Place the second fabric heart shape on top, with right sides facing, sandwiching the ribbon in between the two pieces of fabric. Pin or tack them in place. Sewing a few reverse stitches at the start and finish to stop your seam from unravelling, sew all the way around the edge of the shape, leaving a 2 in. gap on one of the straight edges.

Turn the heart right side out and press it with an iron to define the shape. Pack it with herbs and slip stitch the remaining 2 in. closed. To slip stitch, tuck the raw edges neatly inside and wiggle your needle from left to right, catching the front and back of the pouch as you go (see page 125). Secure with a couple of knots inside the hem.

For the dress on a hanger
Take your coat hanger and snap off most of the plastic arms. You want to leave about 2½ in. of each arm on the hanger so it is a suitable size for the dress (the width of the shoulders of the dress is just about perfect).

Wrap the hook and arms of your hanger in bright ribbon, using craft glue to stick it in place. Sew a couple of stitches at both ends to secure it. **[2 & 3]**

Take the two dress shapes and, on both pieces, fold the neckline of the dress under twice and stitch close to the edge.

Place the fabrics right sides together. Reverse stitching at the start and finish, sew

around the dress shape. Start at one side of the neckline and stop 1¼ in. past the first 'arm' on the side of the dress. Leaving most of the side of the dress open, start stitching 1¼ in. from the bottom of the dress and keep going until you get to the other side of the neckline.

Turn the dress right side out and press to neaten. Slip your covered hanger in through the side opening and take the hook through the open neckline. **[4]**

Add your herbs, then hand-stitch the hole in the side to close it, turning the raw seams under.

Pop it into the wardrobe, inhale and feel your spirits rise.

cushions and pillows

A mountain of cushions in all shapes and sizes are a necessity for rainy afternoon reading, serious slobbing out, and adding decadence and luxury to your bedroom. Make yourself dozens, stack them up like huge marshmallows, then shut the door, sink in and read, daydream or collect your thoughts for an afternoon of blissful coziness.

round cushion

YOU WILL NEED _____

1 Round cushion pad

2 Fabric

3 2 self-cover buttons

4 Needle and thread

5 Pins

6 Fabric scissors

7 Tape measure

8 Sewing machine

9 Newspaper for a pattern

10 Coloring pencil, string and a drawing pin

METHOD

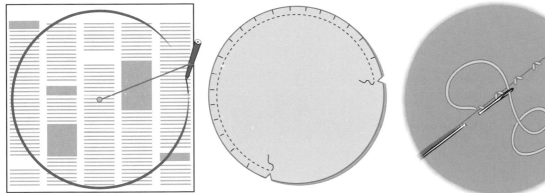

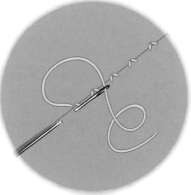

how to slip stitch

Measure the diameter of your cushion pad and add a $^3/_4$ in. seam allowance. Divide this measurement by two.

Place some newspaper on a flat surface. Tie the string to your coloring pencil and secure it in the center of the newspaper with a drawing pin, ensuring that the length of the string between the pencil and drawing pin is exactly the same as the measurement you came to above. Keeping the string taut, draw a circle with the pencil.

Cut out two pieces of fabric, using this paper circle shape as your pattern.

To get the cushion pad into your finished cover, you need to leave

an opening that is a third of the measurement of your cushion's circumference. Either hold a tape measure snugly all the way around the pad and divide that measurement by three, or use this formula: Circumference = Diameter x 3.14 (takes you back to maths class, doesn't it?). My cushion's circumference is 47$^1/_4$ in., so the opening left in the cover needs to be 15$^3/_4$ in. Cut V-shaped notches to denote this section.

Pin the two circles of fabric together, with right sides facing, then stitch a line $^1/_4$ in. in from the edge, two thirds of the way around the circle (from notch to notch).

Snip slits in the seam allowance, outside your stitch line, at $^3/_4$ in.

intervals to keep the fabric from puckering. Then turn the cushion cover right side out.

Pop your cushion pad through the hole. Fold the rest of the seam allowance under, in line with the seams on either side, and sew up the hole using a slip stitch. To do this, work from right to left, securing the thread with a couple of knots hidden inside the hem. Slip stitches are small and virtually invisible – perfect for a tidy finish.

Cover both buttons and attach them by sewing right through the center of the cushion and out the other side. This is much more secure than sewing the buttons onto the surface of the fabric (see page 126) .

covering buttons

This is remarkably quick and satisfying (phew!). It's also very neat if you use self-cover buttons made specifically for the purpose. Just cut a circle of fabric 1/4 in. bigger all round than each button and zigzag-stitch around the edge to stop it from fraying.

Take a needle and thread, tie a knot in the end of the thread to secure it, and sew biggish stitches (about 1/8 in.) just inside the zigzag line all the way around. Place the button in the middle and gently pull the thread until the material gathers snugly around it. Tie a few knots to secure it.

If you are using a self-cover button, slot the back part of the button on to cover the gathering. If you are covering an old button, just secure the gathering with a few more stitches and a couple of knots.

To sew buttons on, use a fairly long needle and thick thread. Tie the end of your thread to the first covered button – a nice reef knot for all you Girl Scouts. Push the needle into the cushion, right through to the other side. Pull firmly and tie the thread onto the second covered button, pulling tight so that the buttons make a dip in the pad. Sew back to the first button, repeat three more times, then tie off again.

Sewing the buttons to each other rather than just the fabric holds them much more firmly in place and causes the fabric to 'dip' in, rather than leaving the buttons 'floating' on the surface.

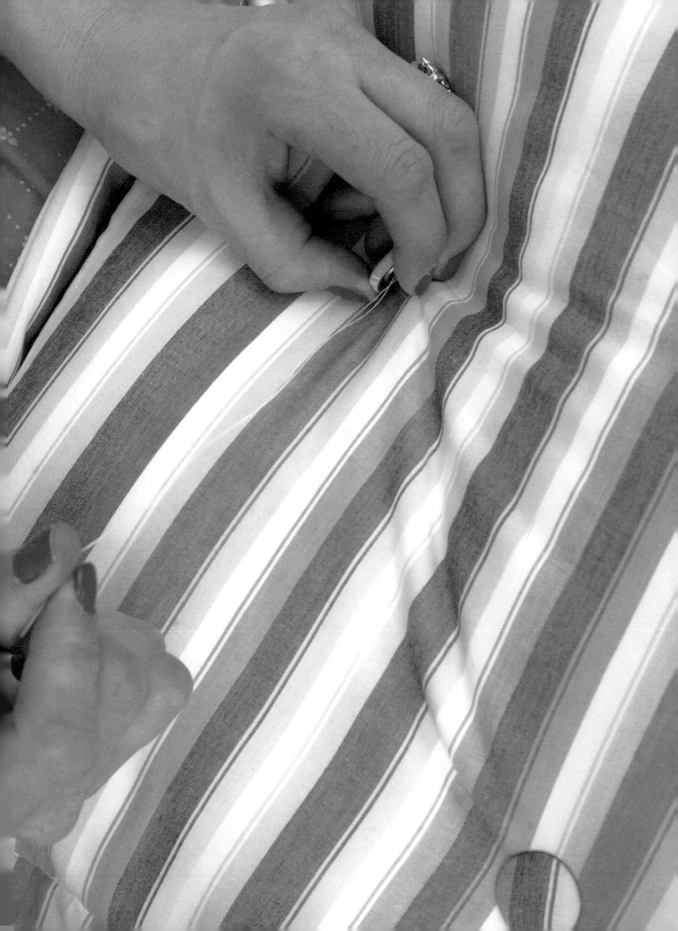

mattress pillow-cushion

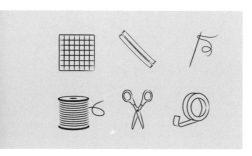

YOU WILL NEED

1. Pillow (18³/₄ x 28³/₄ in. is a standard-sized pillow)
2. 1 yard of fabric
3. 1/2 yard of medium-weight muslin
4. Piece of 2oz polyester batting 3¹/₂ in. larger than your pillow
5. 16 self-cover buttons, all the same size
6. Zipper the same measurement as the width of your pillow (18³/₄ in. is standard)
7. Needle and thread
8. Fabric scissors
9. Tape measure
10. Coloring pencil or tailor's chalk

METHOD

This cushion cover is made to
This cushion cover is made to a larger size than the pillow, then a line of stitching is sewn around the edge to create a flat border. A layer of polyester batting within the border is what makes it stand out, rather than looking deflated.

Measure the size of your pillow. The pillow I used is 18³/₄ x 28³/₄ in.

Cut one piece of fabric 1¹/₂ in. bigger all round than your pillow – this piece is for the top of the cover. I cut my fabric 22 x 32 in. Cut a piece of muslin and a piece of polyester batting to the same size.

Lay the muslin lining on a flat surface, place the batting on top and then the fabric (right side up). Pin the three layers together to hold them in place. Machine-stitch around the edge of these layers and trim away any loose threads and batting.

The back needs to be the same finished length, but you're going to put a zipper in near one end, so you'll need an extra ¹/₂ in. seam allowance in the length. Cut out the back piece in your top fabric. Mine was 22 in. (same width as the front) x 32³/₄ in. (32 in., like the front, plus ³/₄ in. for the zipper seam allowance).

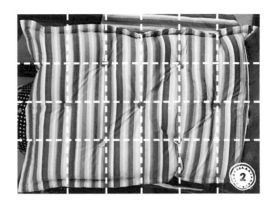

Cut off the last 3 in. of the length of the back of the pillow cover. Place the two parts of the back cover next to each other and work out where the zipper will go. With right sides together and a seam allowance of $1/4$ in., sew a $1/2$ in. in on each side, leaving a gap the length of the zipper. Iron these seams open and press back the seam allowance around the zipper hole. Insert zipper between the two sections (see pages 96–97).

Placing the right sides of your front and back pieces together, pin and then stitch all the way around the outside edge of the pillowcase, $1/4$ in. in from the raw edge.

Make a diagonal cut at the corners to snip away the excess fabric, then undo the zipper and turn the cover right side out. Press flat, making sure that the seam is pushed out to give a neat, straight edge.

To make the flat border on the pillow cover, pin through all the layers, around all the edges of the cover. This will stop them from moving around when you stitch. Sew a line $1 1/4$ in. from the edge of the pillow cover all the way round. [1]

Slot the pillow through the zipper hole and even out the stuffing, so it's not bulging in any direction.

To work out the button spacing, measure the length of the cushion and divide it into six equal segments. Then measure the width and divide that into four. [2] Don't include the border in these measurements. Use pins to indicate the dividing lines and mark the intersecting points with a coloring pencil. These are where the buttons will go.

Cover the buttons and sew them onto your cushion at the positions worked out above. Sew the buttons onto the front and the back at the same time, sewing right through the cushion to attach them to each other, as on page 126.

fantastically frilly pillow

METHOD

These instructions are to make a pillowcase for a pillow measuring 18³/4 x 28³/4 in. The finished case is the perfect fit for standard-sized pillows.

Cut the front piece for your pillowcase to 20³/4 x 30³/4 in., and cut the back piece to 20³/4 x 31¹/4 in. The extra half-inch on the back are for a hem.

Take the back piece, turn ¹/4 in. in at one end, press it, then fold over 2 in. (this is the hem). Press again and sew a line along both edges of this hem.

Cut out the facing for the back of your pillowcase – a piece of fabric measuring 10 x 20³/4 in. Turn one of the long sides under twice as before, press and stitch it down. This is the flap that will keep your pillow inside the cover.

Cut a piece of fabric for the frill, measuring 5³/4 yd. x 5¹/2 in. The measurement of the length is double the outside edge of the pillowcase, plus ³/4 in for a seam allowance. The width (5¹/2 in.) is twice the width of the finished frill (2¹/4 + 2¹/4 in.) plus ¹/4 in.

each side for a seam allowance. Sew the two ends of the frill together, with right sides facing, so the fabric forms a continuous ring. Press the seam, then fold the entire frill in half, widthways, with the wrong sides facing, and press it.

With a long piece of thread and a needle, sew big running stitches (each about ¹/4 in. long) along the raw edge. This is so that you can gather up the fabric to create the frill. Once you have sewn all the way around, tie a large knot in the end to secure and gather up the fabric until the measurement of the circle is 2⁷/8 yd. (the same measurement as the outside edge of your pillowcase). Secure the thread with a couple of back stitches to keep it the correct length, then even out the frills so they are not all bunched up at one end. **[1]**

Pin the frill to the front of the pillowcase, placing the raw edges and right sides of the fabric together. Sew by machine all the way around, leaving a ¹/4 in. seam allowance.

YOU WILL NEED

1 1 yard of fabric
2 Needle
3 Thread
4 Scissors
5 Pillow, measuring 18³/4 x 28³/4 in.

Place the front of the pillowcase right side up and fold the frill in so that the raw edges are visible. Take the facing and place it on top so the right sides are together and the frill is sandwiched between them. Make sure the hemmed edge of the facing is furthest away from the end of the pillow where the frill is joined. Keeping the frill tucked in the middle, sew a line along the width of the pillowcase, joining the front to the facing. [2]

Fold the facing over, to the wrong side of the front piece. You'll now be able to see the frill at the end.

Place the front and back pieces right sides together, with three sides of the frill (the top, the bottom and the end opposite the facing) tucked in inside. Make sure that the hemmed end of the back is at the same end of the pillowcase as the front facing.

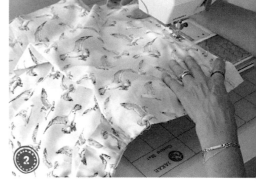

Pin together along the bottom, and sides, leaving the end with facing attached open (this is where you put your pillow in). Make sure that the sides of the piece of the facing are aligned with and pinned into the side seams, too.

Sew around these three sides of your pillowcase. [3] Then stitch around the three sides again with a zigzag stitch to make the seams strong enough for a lifetime of pillow-stuffing. Trim off the excess fabric at the corners (just snip a diagonal line across), so the corners will look neat when you turn the pillowcase right side out.

Turn the pillowcase right side out and pop in a pillow.

trimmed blankets

A giant squashy sofa, a pile of cozy blankets and a good book or the box set of *Desperate Housewives* are essential for hibernating at home. But the humble blanket has been nudged into the storage hinterland by more fashionable comforters of late. Who wants a boring blanket when they can have a crochet cashmere throw with faux chinchilla trimming? OK, I made that up, but look in a Ralph Lauren catalog and you'll get the picture: like lino flooring, people just don't aspire to owning a blanket.

But this misses the point: a blanket is a blank canvas. Trimming is a perfect way to give yours an instant upgrade – and you can be as minimalist or as over the top as you choose. You could even take elements from a fabric used elsewhere in the room to make your blanket coordinate – check out the horses' heads from a Hermès scarf that I used to appliqué. Trimming doesn't require any great skill, and if you've got kids, it makes a perfect rainy afternoon activity. Far more satisfying than watching TV, which, of course, you can all do later on, under your sumptuous, newly desirable blankets.

YOU WILL NEED

1 Blankets
2 Scissors
3 Needle and thread (a sewing machine is handy)
4 Pins
5 Trimmings (ribbons, a chopped-up scarf, pom-pom trim, rickrack)
6 Fabric for appliqué
For blanket stitching the edge
7 A large-eye yarn needle and yarn

METHOD

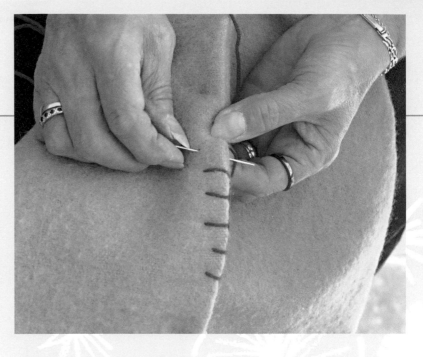

Blanket stitch
The first step is to cut your blanket down to size. Often the reason blankets are left in the cupboard, even when we're cold, is because they're annoyingly big. I snipped these, which were the size of a marquee, to a more manageable 2 yd. square – perfect for curling up under and much more child-friendly. The pink and green blankets I used here were so old they'd felted together, which meant I didn't even need to finish the edges.

If you have a woven blanket, though, like this beige one, edges will start to unravel if you don't do something to prevent it. Blanket stitching is the perfect solution and looks homespun and chic in a contrasting color.

Turn the blanket edge over by ¹/₄ in., pinning as you go to tame it. This will give a soft, firm edge to your blanket and also helps you keep a straight line when stitching. You can hide the starting knot and finishing backstitch within this small hem. Oh, wow! Neatness, too. And now to blanket stitch.

Secure the yarn at the back of the blanket with a couple of knots. Bring the yarn around the outside edge. Insert the needle from the front through to the back ³/₄ in. away from the first stitch and equal distance from the edge of the throw. Bring the needle out at the edge directly below this point, keeping the thread from the previous stitch under the tip of the needle (see diagram below). Pull the needle through until the blanket stitch is snug against the edge of the blanket.

Carry on like this until you get to the end, where you can hide your finishing stitch in the hem. It looks daunting, but each side of this blanket took 10 minutes.

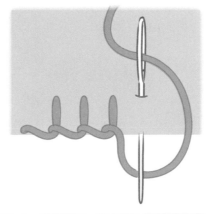

Appliqué

Appliqué will liven up even the dreariest of colors – like this boring beige. You can use any fabric or design for appliqué. Boys might even feign interest if you suggest using pictures of their superheroes, cut from old pillowcases or a T-shirt they've outgrown.

Here, I ironed Vilene onto the back of an old Hermès scarf. Vilene is an adhesive stiffener that gives flimsy fabrics, such as silk, more strength and stops them from fraying.

I know what you're thinking: 'An Hermès scarf, how could she?' Well, in my defence, it was falling to pieces and I hadn't worn it in years. To quote Karl Lagerfeld (describing Claudia Schiffer when he'd decided to drop her for a new muse), '[She] was from another era.' In fact, had my scarf not been a designer piece, it wouldn't have even scraped through recent wardrobe edits. Now, in its new, unique guise, I'm back in love – and especially loving all the compliments it draws.

I cut out the different horses' heads in the pattern and, using a glittery thread, stitched along odd lines to highlight shapes in each.

You don't need to be precise at all – the idea is just to add a little texture and to strengthen the fabric.

The embroidered squares were attached to the blanket by sewing zigzag stitch around the edges on the sewing machine.

For a more formal look, or if you want to sew by hand, iron the edges of the patches under, then stitch them down using a straight stitch.

The rosettes were attached in the same way.

Ribbon bows

Don't feel restricted to edges when it comes to trimming. For the green blanket, my little helper Molly made lots of tiny bows in an acid-lime ribbon. She wanted them to look like butterflies landing on the corner of her blanket.

To secure each bow, just stitch through the center as you sew it onto the blanket.

Now my little helper and I are off for a pot of camomile tea and a snooze … if you don't mind.

Pom-pom trim

This is braid, with little fluffy balls (the small cousin of the pom-poms people use to decorate Christmas trees and children's clothes). You can buy it from trimming specialists, such as drapery supplies in larger fabric stores, and eBay, which is by far the cheapest and often the source for wilder colors.

All you do is zigzag stitch the perimeter of your blanket to stop it from fraying. Then sew the braid on an $1/8$ in. from the edge. When you get to the end, neatly turn the braid under to keep it from fraying.

Attach velvet ribbon, strands of sequins and other braid in the same way.

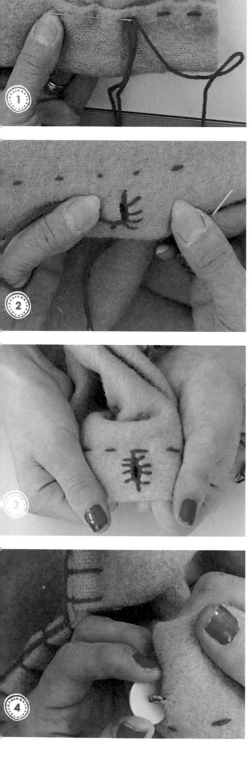

button-up cushion

Using an offcut of my blanket, I made a quick and easy button-back cushion.

YOU WILL NEED

1   Cushion pad (go for 16$^1/_2$ in. square)
2   Blanket offcut
3   Yarn needle and yarn for blanket stitching
4   2 buttons, 1 in. in diameter

METHOD

Cut a piece of blanket 16$^1/_4$ in. square for the front and embellish it as you choose – I appliquéd horses' heads and rosettes to match my blanket.

Cut two more pieces of blanket, both measuring 16$^1/_4$ x 10$^1/_4$ in. These are for the top and bottom sections of the back.

Take the top and bottom sections of the back piece, turn under a 1$^1/_2$ in. hem on each and, using a straight stitch, hand-sew these with contrasting yarn. **[1]**

Now mark where you want your buttons to go. They should be $^1/_4$ in. from the edge and evenly spaced across the width. On the top piece, cut a 1 in. slit at each marking – this will be your buttonhole. Sew around the edge of each buttonhole using tiny blanket stitches ($^1/_8$ in. is fine). **[2 and 3]**

Place the front of your cushion cover right side down and lay the bottom and top parts of the back on top, with right sides facing you; the hems should overlap and the part of the back with buttonholes sewn into the hem should be on top.

Make sure the raw edges are completely aligned with the edge of the front piece of the cushion cover. Pin these together and sew all around the perimeter using blanket stitch.

Sew the buttons onto the hem of the bottom piece of the back cover, directly under the button-holes. **[4]** Squeeze a cushion pad in, and button up to close.

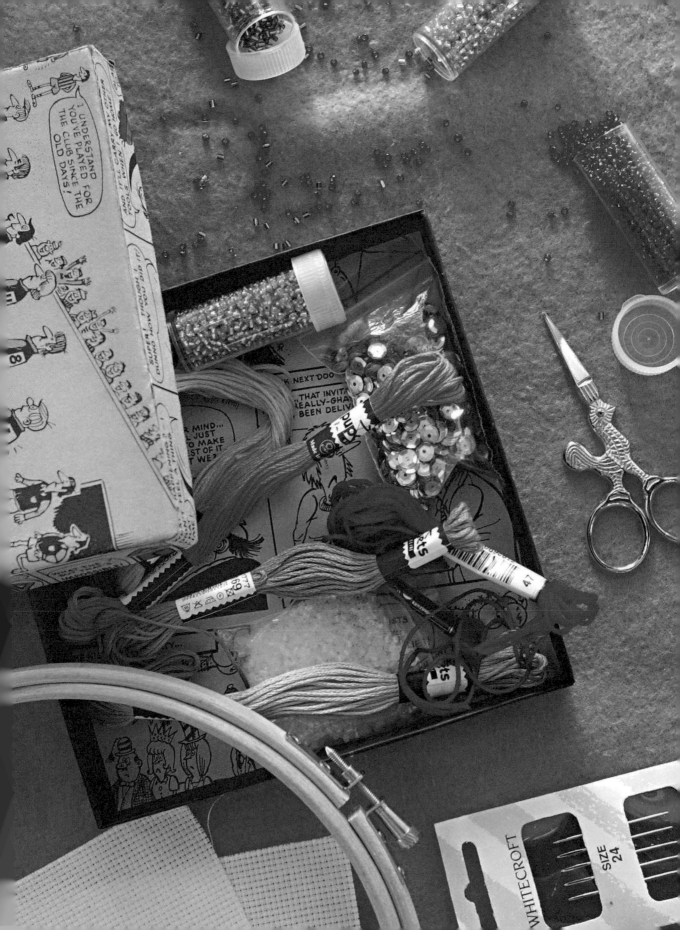

broderie perse bedspread

A trip to the Festival of Quilts – the vast quilting showcase in Birmingham that attracts more than 3,000 entrants a year – inspired this bedspread. I love the look of patchwork and appliqué, but have never had the inclination or precision that you need. And my mom, who has spent the last twenty years making one patchwork quilt, led me to believe that I didn't have the time.

At the festival there were thousands of different styles of quilt – many whipped up in mere months. The exhibition is organized into prize categories, including best geometric, expressive, pictorial, decorative, novice and so on, with trophies, rosettes and – the Holy Grail of the quilting in England – a Bernina sewing machine to be won. It sounds like a strange and esoteric world – stitching meets plane-spotting meets Crufts – but it's all so friendly, despite the coveted Bernina. My companion Stephanie Pettengell, a recent winner in the geometric category, explained that this was in keeping with quilting's social roots. 'Quilters exchange ideas and demonstrate new techniques at the shows to inspire others. There really is no backbiting.' (Though the thought of a patchwork saboteur stitching Superman pillowcases across rival works is so deliciously naughty you almost want it to be true!)

Patchwork, appliqué and broderie perse became the height of fashion in the UK in the seventeenth and eighteenth centuries, when India was the biggest exporter of textiles. The bright animal and bird prints were perfect for cutting out and embellishing other cloths with, and Indian dyes were fixed, so that color wouldn't wash out and run, like British cloths. Talk about exotic. The Indian imports became so popular that in 1701 they were banned, as the government perceived them to be a threat to the UK textile industry. Broderie perse (French for 'Persian embroidery') is the easiest of the techniques – you cut out complete motifs or print designs from one fabric and collage them onto a background fabric. It's an appliqué method, but using whole images or motifs (rather than using plain shapes to make a design) – an instant, easy route to the fashionable Arts and Crafts look. This bedspread should take a day, but enjoy the process and pick it up and put it down as ideas strike you.

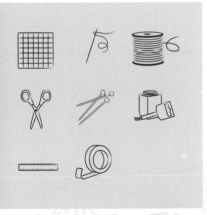

YOU WILL NEED _____

1 Large piece of background fabric (I used an old double blanket)

2 Fabrics featuring designs that you can cut out (I used a reissued Josef Frank design)

3 Contrasting fabric for the border (this works as a frame and ties a haphazard design together; I used Liberty's Lucaya, as the design provides a natural border)

4 Bondaweb (a double-sided bonding web with a paper backing)

5 Trimmings (I used jumbo rickrack and sequins)

6 Fabric scissors

7 Iron and ironing board

8 Tape measure and ruler

9 Colored pencil or tailor's chalk

10 Pins, needles and thread, and a sewing machine if you have one

11 Fabric glue such as Bostick Sew Easy glue

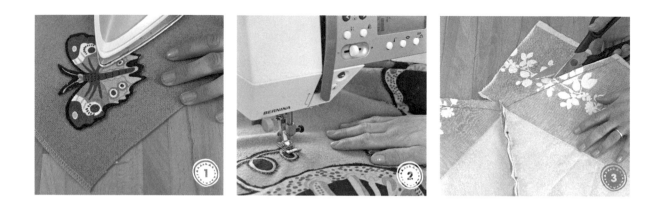

Measure your bed and how far down you'd like the bedspread to hang – remember the border will be extra. For this king-size bedspread my background is 1³/₄ x 2¹/₄ yd. The border adds 3 in. all round, therefore the finished size is 2 x 2¹/₂ yd.

Add ¹/₄ in. seam allowance to your measurement and cut the background fabric to this size.

Take a photo of your fabrics and print a few off on letter-sized paper. These provide small-scale versions of your bedspread to plan your design before you start cutting into your fabric. It's worth spending a bit of time on this and coming up with two or three ideas, cutting out different elements of the pattern to see

which combination looks best against the background cloth.

Iron Bondaweb onto the back of the fabric you're going to cut designs from. You can just apply Bondaweb behind the sections that you intend to cut out. When the fabric and Bondaweb have cooled, gently peel off the paper backing. If the Bondaweb comes with it, it has not yet fused properly, so iron again, pressing down hard and for between 30 and 60 seconds. Bondaweb prevents fraying, so you can leave edges raw, rather than having to turn them under. This will save you a lot of time and hassle and you can tell everyone that raw edges are modern and fashionable, which they are.

Cut out the design motifs from your printed fabric and place them on your background fabric, right side up (as per paper version of your design). Iron them in place – the Bondaweb will fuse these pieces of fabric to your background. [1]

Once all the pieces are stuck in place, sew around the edges of each, using a straight stitch. [2] Bernina machines are great for this as they have a special freestyle setting that lets you zoom around curves and corners, without stopping and starting. You will be very glad you used Bondaweb, as you won't need to turn the fiddly edges under.

Cut a border for your bedspread. This should be double the width

you want the finished border to be plus ¼ in. on each side. You will need 4 strips: two the length of your bedspread plus 15½ in. and two the width plus 15½ in. The 15½ in. is for miter-ing each corner (7¾ in. at each end).

Place your background fabric right side up and the border pieces WRONG side up. Pin together, ¼ in. from the edge. Sew all the way around, ¼ in. from the edge.

Iron all the raw edges up into the border – so once you fold your border over and sew it, they will be sandwiched and hidden inside. At each corner draw a diagonal line from the corner of your background fabric to the centre of your border (the fold

line); sew this up. Then fold the border over, along the central line, and draw a mirror image of the diagonal line on the second half of the border. Cut, ¼ in. from the line, [3] and sew this line up.

Trim away the excess fabric next to the seam. Turn the border out and iron it flat.

Fold the raw edge neatly under (into the border), pin it, then sew with a straight stitch and close to the fold using your sewing machine. [4] Iron again.

Using fabric glue, stick your trims down. [5] Then sew them in place with matching thread, either by hand or machine. I went for a real Arts and Crafts

Quilting

To quilt your bedspread, buy some batting and backing fabric (a sheet will do). Both need to be the same size as your background fabric. Quilting will hide all the working on the back and make the bedspread warmer. As I used a blanket for my background fabric, I decided against it – let's face it, we're not living in the North Pole. Annoyingly, this means I can never enter it into the Festival of Quilts competition (a quilt, by definition, is two layers of cloth filled with stuffing and stitched together).

If you decide to quilt your bedspread, when you get to joining the border, simply place the backing fabric, then wadding, then top fabric on top of one other and sew all three into the border.

Top tip

• Always wash your fabric before you start – if the dye runs or the fabric shrinks afterwards, you'll have ruined everything.

Check out the Festival of Quilts at www.twistedthread.com.

tie-top
curtains

Making curtains is easy, but having them made for you is so cheap that there's little point in doing it yourself – unless you make something so show-stoppingly lavish that it would be too expensive to buy or too much hassle to explain. The trick, though, is to spend more time soaking up the compliments than making the curtains themselves.

Imagine glittering brash-luxe drapes trailing to the floor, with the bespoke kind of quality (batting, hand-finishing and the like) that you'd expect from companies such as Mulberry or Designers Guild. You want something that screams boudoir, individuality and one high-maintenance owner – without the workload. Here, I've tried to minimize the work by making a very easy curtain, while leaving acres of time for styling. Have fun and don't be surprised when commissions for your DIY drapery start rolling in.

YOU WILL NEED _____

1   Fabric
2   Medium-weight Dormette or Bump interlining (woven interlining that adds thickness but does not sag like batting, which is unstructured)
3   Lining fabric
4   Glitzy trimmings (such as sequins, fringed beading and ribbons)
5   Curtain weighting tape, the width of the curtain
6   Matching thread, needle and sewing machine
7   Curtain pole
8   Craft glue
9   Iron and ironing board
10 Fabric scissors

METHOD

I think curtains always look best if they flow to the floor, so don't mess about with windowsills. Measure from the top of your window to the floor and add 8³/4 in. This will make curtains about 2³/4 in. longer than your window to floor measurement, depending on where you attach the curtain pole and how tight you tie the ties at the top – perfect for getting a couple of luxurious folds as the curtains hit the floor. For the width, measure the width of the window. Each side of your curtains should measure the same as the entire width of the window (so if you added the measurements of both curtains, the total would be double the width of the window).

Cut the fabric to the required size for each curtain. If your fabric isn't wide enough, join widths together with a flat seam, as close to the outside edge as possible.

Cut the lining fabric 4 in. narrower and 1¹/2 in. shorter than the two pieces of curtain fabric. Then fold the bottom of

the lining under by ³/4 in. and under again by 1¹/2 in. and stitch this hem down.

Cut a piece of interlining that is 2³/4 in narrower than your curtain fabric and 4 in. shorter.

Lay your main curtain fabric flat. Fold the bottom of the fabric under by ³/4 in. and under again by 1¹/2 in., pin it in place, then iron the fold and stitch it down.

Now get decorating. I enhanced very tasteful stripes with lines of sequins and ribbon. I glued these with a thin strip of craft glue (it dries clear), then organized a takeaway night with girlfriends where we gossiped and each hand-stitched a few strands of sequins down before we'd had too much to drink. Using something sparkly but tonally similar to add texture to an existing pattern on a fabric looks slick, without taking the magpie thing too far. For the trimming, you can use anything that takes your fancy – feathers, pom-poms or fringing, for example – and it's worth trying

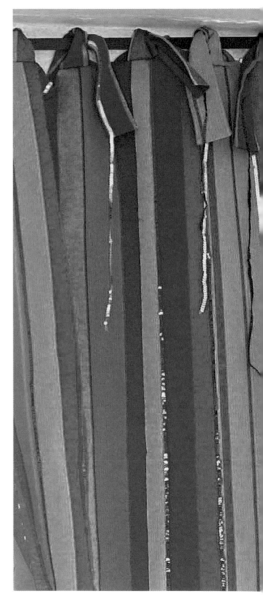

something unexpected. Windows are the single most important feature in a room, so aim for gasps of 'WOW' not 'whatever'.

To make the ties, which will hold the curtains to your curtain pole, cut a long strip of your main fabric 4³/4 in. wide, fold it in half widthways, with right sides facing, press and cut into pieces 9³/4 in. long. You need sufficient strips for two ties at each end and two ties about every 4 in. or so in between.

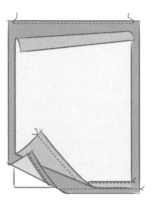

With right sides still together, sew seams across one short edge and down the length of each 9³/4 in. strip you've just cut, sewing ¹/4 in. in from the raw edges. Snip diagonally across the corner on each piece to cut away the excess fabric, then iron the seams open.

Turn each tie right side out, using a ruler or a piece of dowelling to push the tube of fabric through itself, making sure to poke the corners out. Iron the ties flat.

Place the curtain fabric right side down. Place the interlining on top and line up the raw edges at the top. The interlining is 2¹/2 in. narrower than the curtain fabric, so make sure it's placed

centrally (that's 1¹/4 in. from each side). Join the two fabrics at the top with a line of stitching a ¹/8 in. from the raw edge.

Lay the fabric and interlining on a flat surface with the curtain fabric facing up. Place the lining centrally on top of it, right side down, and align the top edges (see above left).

Pin the sides of your lining and top fabric together, aligning the raw edges. (The lining fabric is a little narrower than your top fabric, so that the top fabric will fold around to the back of the curtain, giving a neater finish than if the side seams were visible.) Stitch down the length of each side edge, ¹/4 in. in (see above, center). Do not stitch

along the top or bottom hem.

Still working on the wrong side, shake the curtain out, then lay it perfectly flat and smooth it with your hands, rolling 1 in. (not including the ¹/4 in. seam allowance) of the main fabric in to the wrong side, towards the lining. Your fold line should be in line with the edge of the interlining, all the way down.

Once the side seams are placed correctly, sew up the top edge of the curtain, joining all the fabrics by stitching a line ¹/4–¹/2 in. from the top all the way across (see above right). Trim the raw edges to a ¹/8 in. from the seam.

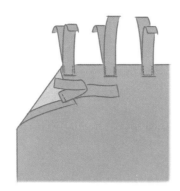
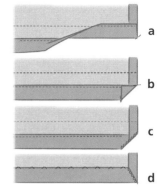

Turn the curtains right side out and press the top and rolled-back sides.

Pin your pressed ties to the top edge of the curtain. You want to place two (one on the back and one on the front) at each end, and two at regular intervals (of about 4 in.) in between – work out the nearest equal interval to 4 in. for your curtain width.

As you pin the ties, the finished edge should be pointing up while the raw edges should be folded neatly under and pinned to the top of the curtain, about 2 in. down from the edge (see above). Pin one tie from each pair to the front and one to the back, making sure they are directly on top of each other

with the top edge of the curtain sandwiched between. Next you'll sew straight through all the layers, attaching both ties at the same time.

Sew a 'U' shape around each set of ties, joining the front and back tie simultaneously.

To false miter the curtain hem With a pin, mark 10 in. from the bottom on each side of your curtain fabric – this should be in line with where the interlining and lining finish.

Iron a fold all the way along this line; this is your hem line (see diagram a).

Fold the corners in diagonally, so the point of the corner is

perfectly in line with where the curtain fabric meets the lining (see diagram b). Place a pin at either end of your diagonal line. Sew a zigzag stitch just outside the diagonal line. Snip off the excess fabric, outside the stitching (see diagram c). Then iron the diagonal line under $1/4$ in.

Fold the hem up and iron it. Place a strip of curtain weighting tape along the hem line and stitch it in place at either end. Slip-stitch the diagonal hem sides to the main curtain fabric that you rolled round from the front (see diagram d), then hand-sew the top of the hem, attaching it to the lining and interlining, but not going right through to the main curtain fabric at the front.

reupholstered ottoman

Transforming old furniture with new upholstery creates instant results. You can pick ottomans up practically anywhere and, thanks to their blocky shape, they're perfect for showing off stylish fabrics, such as this muted Missoni stripe. You don't need much fabric and they're great for storage – far easier on the eye than a stack of IKEA boxes, too.

1   Ottoman
2   Fabric (Missoni, Osborne & Little and Neisha Crosland do wonderful patterns, or rummage through textile bins at thrift stores; 1970s curtains in a new context can look surprisingly chic)
3   2 oz. polyester batting
4   2 in.-thick foam
5   Mulin or fire-retardant barrier fabric (if your fabric does not reach current safety regulations – see note below)
6   Fabric to cover the inside of the lid (a plain canvas is ideal)
7   Foam adhesive spray (buy this from a foam supplier)
8   Hand-held staple gun
9   ¹/₂ in. (13mm) upholsterer's tacks
10 Flat-ended screwdriver (to lever out tacks and staples)
11 Hammer (a magnetic one if you're prone to dropping tacks)

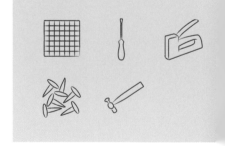

Ask your fabric supplier whether the materials you would like to work with conform to current fire regulations. Some fabrics, such as cotton and wool, are inherently fire retardant. Those that aren't can be used with a fire-retardant barrier cloth or have a backing fused on, so they meet regulations. Ask your supplier for advice.

Remove the old covering from the ottoman by levering out tacks and staples. Do this by placing the flat end of a screw-driver under the head of the tack or the center of the staple and knock the handle gently with a hammer. Push in line with the grain of the wood and they should come out easily. Remove the old foam, discard and unscrew the lid if it's hinged. **[1]**

Measure the top of the ottoman. Note this measurement, then add $3/4$ in. all round (adding $11/2$ in. total to the width measurement and $11/2$ in. in total to the length). Ask your foam supplier to cut you a piece of 2 in.-thick foam to this measurement. The extra $1/2$ in. will allow for the upper edge of foam to fold down over the

edge, creating a nice curve once you secure the fabric over it. Do ask your foam supplier to cut the foam for you – you can using a bread knife, but it'll be as precise as a dog chewing it.

Spray lots of foam adhesive onto the ottoman lid and onto one side of the piece of foam, then place the sticky side of the foam centrally on the ottoman lid.

Cut a piece of polyester batting 2 in. bigger all around than the measurement of the ottoman lid. **[2]** Staple the batting along one of the long sides on the underside of the lid. Then bring it over the top of the ottoman and, holding it very tight, staple the opposite side. **[3]** Staple the two ends in the same way. Chop

away the excess batting from the corners, then staple down the trimmed-down edges.

Measure across the curve of the foam, which is now covered in batting, and cut your covering fabric $3/4$ in. bigger all round than this measurement. Make sure you include the part of the pattern that you want showing on the lid, and cut the fabric on the straight grain (in line with the edge, or selvedge, of the fabric).

Turn the edge of the fabric under by $1/4$ in all round and iron. Place the fabric on top of your ottoman and attach it with one tack in the center of each side underneath the lid; secure both long sides first, then the

ends, pulling the fabric tight as you go. Working out from the central tack towards the corners, secure the rest of each side using tacks or a staple gun, whichever you find easiest (I prefer staples as they're more precise and quicker to pop in). [4] Make sure you pull the fabric taut from side to side and end to end as you go, and space the tacks or staples evenly and close together. Stop 2 in. from each corner.

Once the four sides are secure, there will still be loose excess fabric at the corners. Pull the center of this excess taut and, holding it tightly, staple a few times, 1/4 in, on the underside of the lid. Once you've done this you should be left with an equal quantity of loose fabric on each side of the stapled center. Taking the excess fabric on one

of the short sides of the ottoman, pull it tight and, making sure that the fabric is taut, staple it to the underside of the lid.

Fold the remaining side in a neat vertical pleat. To do this, hold the fabric taut and straight out. Fold the excess under (it should fall under easily in a 'V' shape). [5] Pull the fabric straight down to the underside of the lid, creating a neat pleat. Still holding the fabric, tap the pleat gently with a hammer for a professional flat finish. Then secure on the underside with a few staples. The pleat may take a couple of goes, but getting it right and completely straight makes all the difference. Repeat for the other corners, then staple any gaps between the corners and where you

finished attaching fabric on each of the sides.

Cut a piece of plain canvas 1/4 in bigger all round than the inside of the lid. Turn the edges under by 3/4 in and iron. Staple the fabric neatly to the inside of the lid, covering all the tacks or staples and raw edges. [6]

wallpapered drawers

Wallpapering furniture offers so much more scope than dreary color-blocking with paint. Designers do it – and charge handsomely for their work – but, with a little precision on your part and an eye for a stylish pattern, you can easily achieve the same results yourself. This project is perfect for turning dull (but handily flat-surfaced) 1980s furniture into something eye-poppingly chic. Here, I'm working on a chest and just papering the drawers, but you could apply the same processes to tabletops or wardrobes (papering panels looks especially good). A perfect use for vintage paper that you don't have much of, or a great excuse to splash out on a small quantity of the designer stuff.

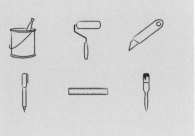

YOU WILL NEED

1 Chest of drawers (go for a plain design with flat drawer fronts – a cheap flat-pack chest is ideal)
2 Wallpaper (you'll need a few yards, as you have to match the pattern from drawer to drawer. Huge abstract prints tend to work very well for this application. Look at Cole & Son's Contemporary Collection, Neisha Crosland's brilliant 'Hollywood Grapevine' and Graham & Brown's less expensive monochrome designs for ideas.)
3 Paint that matches at least one element of the wallpaper
4 Sandpaper
5 Damp cloth
6 Small paint roller
7 Craft knife and cutting mat
8 Pen or pencil and metal ruler
9 Spray mount and nail scissors
10 Wallpaper paste (or use craft glue if you're applying paper to painted furniture)
11 Wallpaper brush and a squeegee
12 Clean, damp sponge
13 Acrylic sealant
14 Paintbrush

METHOD

Remove any knobs and take the drawers out of your chest. Lightly sand – just enough to give a slightly rough surface – then wipe with a damp cloth. Keeping your drawers in the right order (top one first), place them in a line with the drawer front facing upwards.

Paint the rest of your chest in a color that suits the paper you are using on the drawers. (You could paper it, but this is fiddly and a lot of hassle for little more return than you'll get from just papering the drawers). Use a roller for painting, so you get an ultra-flat finish, which will work better with the printed surface of the wallpaper.

Place the wallpaper on a large, flat surface and unravel a length to look at the pattern. If you have narrow drawers (the same width as the paper or less) you can work vertically. But if your drawers are wider than the width of the paper, as mine are, work horizontally, otherwise you'll have joins in the middle of each drawer, which will look awful. Some graphic patterns

may look OK either way, but a floral or pictorial print won't work horizontally, so it's best to choose a paper that suits your furniture from the outset.

Decide which part of the pattern you want to use. I'm using a huge-scale Cole & Son paisley here and can only fit one paisley across the entire width of my drawer, so it makes sense for me to start at the beginning of one of the paisleys. If you have a stripe or small pattern it won't matter so much. Using a sharp craft knife, cut a length of the paper, which contains the part of pattern you want to use, an inch wider than your top drawer. If you're working horizontally, you'll beable to get at least two

drawers from this piece of paper – possibly more, depending on the height of each drawer. This is good news, as cutting these one on top of the other means you don't need to match up the pattern, as it's already done for you. Draw around the top drawer. [1] Then, directly below this outline, draw around the next drawer down, making sure that the sides of each line up exactly. Also, be sure to place the second drawer right underneath the first (don't leave a gap in between them, or there will be a glitch in your pattern).

Fit as many consecutive drawers on the paper as you can. You'll cut the rest in a minute.

Using a metal ruler and craft knife, cut out your first couple of outlines on a cutting mat. Don't use scissors – you need more precision. Hold the cut-outs against their corresponding drawer fronts. They should fit perfectly, but if they are slightly bigger, spray the back of the paper with a little repositionable spray mount, put the wallpaper in place on the drawer front and trim the edge using nail scissors. If the furniture is old, the edge of the drawer may not be completely straight, thanks to years of being knocked, so you might need to cut off tiny slivers to compensate. If you are further out, place the drawer face down on the craft mat and cut away excess paper using a craft knife.

Unravel some more wallpaper. Find where the next drawer edge needs to be to match the pattern with your previous drawer and cut your next piece of paper. This time, cut it the same width as the previous outlines. Continue in this way and make sure that you keep your drawers and paper pieces in the correct order. **[2]**

Brush or sponge wallpaper paste onto the back of the wallpaper pieces, as directed on the paste packet.

Place the pasted wallpaper pieces onto the drawers (they should still be in a line with the drawer fronts facing up). **[3]** Start from the top and keep the drawers in the correct order – sometimes, even if the drawers look the same size, there might be less than an inch difference between them, so it can be a real pain if you mix them up. Carefully slide the paper into place and adjust.

Lightly brush with the wallpaper brush or a squeegee to remove any air pockets and patches of excess glue – though don't worry too much about the bumps of glue, as the paper will flatten out as the moisture in the paste evaporates.

Wipe away any excess paste with a clean, damp (but not wet) sponge and allow to dry thoroughly.

Leave the drawers overnight to dry completely. Then, using a clean, dry brush, paint them with clear acrylic sealant. Four to five coats will make it robust enough for everyday use.

upholstered chair with box cushion

A decorative chair is a perfect statement piece for the bedroom and you can add verve by upholstering yourself. Look at the revamped Victorian and Charles Eames classics in Paul Smith's new furniture collection. He takes chairs – often very ornate ones – and gives them new life with startling, unexpected material. Get inspired. Find a forlorn gem of your own. With a few tacks and some snazzy fabric you can create your own designer masterpiece.

The key to revamping an old piece is to find furniture that's comfortable, that's an appealing shape and that's structurally sound. Ignore anything with cracks in the wood – especially at corner joints – although if a joint is just loose it can easily be reglued.

You'll find that hunting for a piece is half of the fun. Plan a mini-break to neighborhood yard sales, flea markets, look in your parent's loft – or, better still, your grandmother's – try local reclamation yards (à la Paul Smith), auction houses or log on to eBay. Also consider farmers' markets. Traditionally places that you'd visit to buy cows and sheep, these have now diversified to include house clearances and furniture sales, as farmers sell up and move on to pastures new.

YOU WILL NEED

1   Framed chair
2   Fabric (look at Neisha Crosland, Florence Broadhurst, or rummage through thrift stores textile bins)
3   4oz polyester padding (the same size as the chair back); 2oz polyester batting (3/4 in. bigger all round than the top of the cushion)
4   Muslin (strong cotton used to cover padding under the final fabric)
5   Burlap (used to hold the stuffing or padding in place)
6   Hammer and flat-ended screwdriver, to lever out tacks and staples
7   Hand-held staple gun
8   3/8 inch (10mm) and 1/2 inch (13mm) upholsterer's tacks (3/8 inch are used for the burlap and muslin layers; 1/2 inch for the top fabric where there are more layers to go through)
9   Braid (sufficient to trim your chair), and craft glue or a hot glue gun
10 Iron and ironing board
11 Fabric scissors

METHOD

Strip down your chair. [1] It's important that you remove each layer individually and keep them safe. Some parts you'll be able to reuse, others you'll need to draw around for a pattern. You should start by picking off the trim. Then remove the fabric layers – drive out tacks by placing the flat end of your screwdriver under the head of the tack and gently knock the handle with a hammer. Do this in line with the grain of the wood and they'll come out easily.

Once your chair is stripped, decide whether or not to repaint or stain the wood. This is the time to do it, if you want to, and remember to rough up the surface first with sandpaper.

Using the piece of fabric that covered the back as a pattern, cut out a new piece in your chosen fabric. [2] You want enough fabric to fold a $3/4$ in. hem all the way around – if the previous back piece looks too small to turn back a $3/4$ in. hem, adjust the size you cut accordingly.

Then cut a piece of burlpa and a piece of muslin to the same size as this new piece of fabric. The burlap holds your padding in place and the muslin works as a barrier between the top fabric and the padding. I'm using the burlap that was already in my chair, which happens to be a little bigger than my new fabric, but this makes no difference.

Note: For the following steps you can staple or tack. Tacking is the traditional method, but stapling is used interchangeably in modern upholstery. It is just as strong and also very precise, as you can staple closer together which creates a more even pull on the fabric.

Place the burlap on top of the wrong side of your outer fabric. With the burlap still facing you, position the top edges of the fabrics against the back of the chair frame, so that the right side of the fabric is visible from the back of the chair. Fold a $3/4$ in. hem forward and tap a tack into the center of the top frame. [3] Directly below, pull the fabrics taut, turn up your hem and

have used elsewhere on the chair and mount the panel (in my case, the tapestry) on top of it by pinning it on perfectly flat, then stitching around the edge. Doing this ensures that the tension of the fabric across the back of the chair remains even, which won't be the case if you patch together different densities of weave.

Sew a zigzag stitch all the way around this back piece. Your stitch line should be just outside where you want to tack the fabric to the chair (about $1/2$ in. from the edge of the fabric). Before you start, check where the stitch line should be by holding the fabric to your chair back and inserting pins to guide you where to sew. Once you've stitched the zigzag, trim your fabric down to $1/8$ in. outside the stitching.

Press the zigzag stitching under. Remember to keep the iron temperature suitable for your fabric. If you are concerned, place a cotton tea towel on top before you iron – much better than burning your fabric.

knock a tack into the center of the bottom frame. Do the same in the center of each side, making sure you pull the fabrics tight to prevent any sagging – otherwise you'll have to start again.

Working outwards from the middle of the top to the sides, fold your hem and hammer in more tacks, leaving $1/4$–$1/2$ in. spaces in between each tack. Do the same at the bottom, then each side, remembering to pull the fabrics taut as you go.

Cut a layer of batting, the same size as the back but without the $3/4$ in. hem turning. I used the batting that was already in my chair. If yours is intact, there's no reason why you shouldn't either.

Take your muslin, cut snips into the $3/4$ in. seam allowance and tuck the seam allowance around the batting. (The snips make it easier to tuck the muslin around the curved edge.) Attach both layers, using your staple gun, and pull opposing sides taut as you attach them. [4]

Cut your top fabric for the front of the back, with a $3/4$ in. seam allowance. Use the original top fabric that you removed from the chair as a pattern. For the back of my chair, I was desperate to use an old tapestry I'd found in a local market, which was smaller than the back of my chair. If you have a piece of treasured fabric that isn't quite big enough, cut a piece of top fabric in the same fabric that you

Hold the fabric to the top of the back frame, with the right side facing you. Making sure the hem is still turned under as you go, secure either with tacks or staples as close to the folded edge as you can ($1/8$ in. is ideal). Use the same method as with the outer back fabric: tap a tack into the center of the top first. Then, directly below, pull the fabric taut and, checking the hem is still turned under, knock a tack into the center of the bottom frame. Do the same in the center of each side, again keeping as close to the edge as possible and pulling the fabric tight as you go. Fill in the gaps, adding tacks or staples, working from the middle of the top out to the sides, and so on.

Glue the very end of your decorative braid under using craft glue or a hot glue gun. Then, starting under an arm or somewhere else relatively discreet, glue on the braid in a continuous strip all the way around (I find a glue gun easier and more precise than craft glue, but you can use either).

The braid should cover all the tacks, staples and the edge of the fabric, which is why it's so important to secure the fabric as close to the edge of the chair frame as possible. Pull the braid slightly taut as you work to give a neat, flat finish. [5] When you near your starting point, leave $1/2$ in. extra, then cut the braid, turn the end under and glue it down. [6]

I then added further surface texture to the tapestry, by sewing on seed beads and sequins to highlight elements of the picture. [7]

Upholstered arms and sides of framed chairs can be done using the same method as above.

box cushion with piping

YOU WILL NEED

1. 4 in.-thick foam cut to the size of the seat (have it cut square, even if the seat tapers a little)
2. Fabric to match your chair and fire-retardant barrier fabric if the outer fabric does not conform to current fire regulations
3. Zipper, 2 in. shorter than the measurement of the back of the cushion
4. 1 gauge of piping cord, long enough to go around the perimeter of the top of the cushion
5. Matching thread, needle and sewing machine
6. Tape measure
7. Fabric scissors
8. Iron and ironing board

Measure the seat area of your chair, and have a piece of foam cut to size. It's better to go a tiny bit larger (about $1/2$ in.), rather than smaller. This way the cushion will fill fit snugly between the arm rests and rails and they will hold it in place. Much better than having it slip around.

Cut two pieces of fabric, $3/4$ in. bigger than the top of the foam shape, for the top and bottom of your cushion cover. Cut the corners ever so slightly curved, rather than at right angles, which are much harder to sew piping around.

To create the welt – that's the panel of fabric that gives the cushion its depth – measure the depth of your foam (that's 4 in.) and add $3/4$ in. for a seam allowance. This will be the width of the two welt pieces that you cut. To get the length, measure the front and one side of your foam pad (that is, half the perimeter) and add $3/4$ in. to this measurement. Cut two pieces of fabric to these measurements and snip V-shaped notches at the points that should match up with each corner.

NB: Even if the seat of your chair tapers a little towards the back, a rectangular or

square cushion will still be fine. If your seat tapers a lot, though, and you have had your foam cut accordingly, measure the back of the foam and then one side and cut the second part of the welt according to these measurements.

Ensure that the pattern in your fabric – or the nap, if you are using velvet – is the right way up. Sew the two welt pieces together to form a ring, leaving $1/4$ in. unsewn at the top and bottom of each seam (see diagram a, next page). Stitch your seams $1/4$ in. from the raw edges of the fabric, then press them open with an iron.

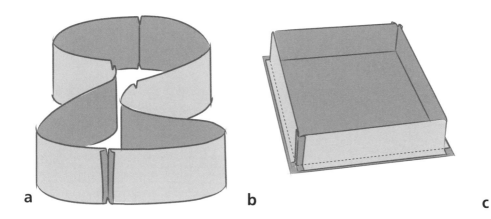

a

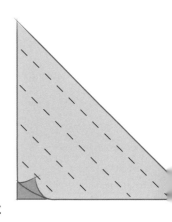

b

c

Place the bottom edge of the welt around the perimeter of the bottom of your cushion cover, with right sides together. Align the notches with the corresponding corners and pin together, $1/4$ in. from the edges. Keep the raw edges aligned and pin all the way around, $1/4$ in. in from the edges.

Place a zipper in the seam at the back, between the welt and the bottom piece of the cushion cover. Sew this in as per the instructions on pages 96–97. Then undo the zipper.

Stitch the other three sides of the welt to the bottom piece of

the cushion cover, matching the vertical seams in your welt with the corners of the bottom piece (see diagram b).

To make the piping
You can buy piping, which looks great in contrasting colors, or make it, which is marginally more hassle but means you can choose the fabric.

To make piping, you need to cut several diagonal strips of fabric. Cutting the fabric on the bias makes it a bit stretchy, which is useful for going around corners. This uses up quite a lot of fabric, so if your material is expensive, consider using a less expensive,

contrasting fabric for the piping. To cut a bias strip, roll out a length of cloth and fold the fabric diagonally so that a straight edge is in line with the selvedge.

Iron this fold flat, and cut lots of parallel bias strips 1 in. wide, using this fold line as a guide (see diagram c).

To join your strips, pin the ends together at right angles to each other, with right sides together. Sew, then trim off the excess fabric and press the seams open (see diagram d).

METHOD

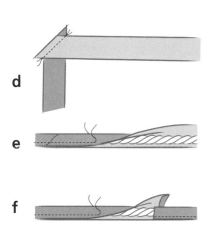

Join enough strips to go all the way around the perimeter of the top of the cushion.

Lay your bias strip right side down and place the piping cord in the middle of the strip. Fold the fabric over the cord, match up the raw edges and sew a line as close to the cord as you can (see diagram e). If you are using a sewing machine, a zipper foot will help you sew closer to the cord than a normal foot. [1]

Pin the piping to the right side of the top piece of the cushion cover. You want your seam line to be 1/4 in. in from the edge and close to the cord. At each corner, cut slits into the seam allowance and ease the piping around the

curve, then pin it in place (this will be easy as your corners are slightly curved, rather than at right angles).

Starting at the center back, stitch the piping in place. Don't do a reverse stitch, just go straight on around the cushion top.

When you get to where you started, unpick 1/4 in. of stitching at the beginning of the piping cord, pull the cover back and snip off 1/4 in. of cord. Tuck the other end of the piping cord inside this fabric sleeve, fold the edges back to neaten and hand-sew in place (see diagram f).

Pin the top piece of the cushion cover to the top edge of the welt, 1/4 in. from the raw edges and matching the corners with the seams in the welt.

Stitch together, as close to the cord as possible, using a zipper foot if you are working on a sewing machine. Turn your new cushion cover right side out and squeeze the foam through the zipper hole.

Cut a piece of batting 1 in. bigger than your piece of foam, and slide it onto the top of the foam, neatly smoothing over the corners and sides to give a smooth curve to the edges of the cushion.

Bathroom

create a bathing haven

laundry bag

The main reasons bathrooms look messy are because nothing coordinates and dirty socks and pants are left strewn over the floor. Make a few accessories in matching fabrics and you're halfway to bathroom harmony. You'll also have something considerably more stylish than the utilitarian cream canvas sacks that scream 'I shop at IKEA, just like everyone else!' A laundry bag is quick to make, keeps washing out of sight and, assuming you'll make something else in matching fabric, like the Roman blind on the next page, it will pull the room together.

YOU WILL NEED

1   2 yards fabric
2   2 yards medium-weight muslin for the lining
3   Matching thread
4   Needle and sewing machine, if you have one
5   Fabric scissors
6   Tape measure
7   Dowelling
8   Safety pin
9   Iron and ironing board
10 Cord for drawstring (optional)

METHOD

Cut two pieces of fabric 26 x 22 in. This measurement allows for $^{1}/_{2}$ in. seam allowance. Cut two pieces of muslin lining fabric to the same size.

Cut a notch (the technical term for a little slit $^{1}/_{3}$ in.) 4 in. down from the top of your two pieces of fabric, on both sides. The point of a notch is so you can match up the sides. Do the same with the lining.

Place one piece of lining on a flat surface and the two pieces of outer fabric on top, right sides together. Put the other piece of lining on top. Make sure that all the notches are aligned, then pin the fabrics together.

Leaving the top 4 in. unsewn, sew all the way around from one notch to the other, $^{1}/_{2}$ in. from the edge. Then sew a zigzag stitch just outside this line to prevent the raw edges from fraying. [1]

Now, take the fabric and lining above the notch (you need to keep the front and the back pieces separate for this bit). Using the $^{1}/_{2}$ in. seam allowance, turn the sides of both the front and back pieces inside twice and sew, neatening the edges for your drawstring channel.

Fold the top edges inwards $^{1}/_{4}$ in. and press to neaten, then fold down the front and back pieces to the inside of your laundry bag and pin them in line with your notch. This creates a channel for the drawstring.

Working on the front and back of the bag in turn, sew along this fold line from one side to the other, then sew a parallel line $^{3}/_{4}$ in. above the first. Sew over both of these lines again for extra strength. [2]

Sew up the little openings that are left, just above your drawstring channel, using slip stitches.

For the drawstring

The quickest option is to buy cord from a fabric or craft store – if you want to do this, choose a cord that's no less than $1/8$ in. in diameter. The alternative is to make your own drawstring, which I think looks much better. I used the same fabric as I used for the bag, but contrasting fabric looks good, too. In fact, now that I've made a blind with a seagull trim (see the following pages), I'm tempted to make a seagull-print drawstring for this bag, too – far more chic.

Cut a piece of fabric 1 yard long and $2^1/2$ in. wide. Fold it in half lengthways, with the right sides facing.

Pin the edges together and sew along one end, then sew all the way along the length, stopping $1/2$ in. from the other end. **[1]**

Snip diagonally across the corner you've sewn up, to cut away the excess fabric, then iron the seam open.

Use a piece of dowelling to poke the tube of fabric through itself, shimmying the drawstring over the dowelling until it's turned right side out. **[2]**

Once the drawstring is turned right side out, iron it flat, then tuck the raw edges at the open end to the inside, and slip-stitch the end closed. **[3]**

Repeat the above, so you have two drawstrings.

Feed one drawstring through the channel on the front of your bag and the other through the channel on the back. Use a safety pin on one end of the drawstring to help you feed it through the channel. Tie the two drawstrings together at the sides. **[4]**

Hang your hip new creation off a hook, a radiator or the door and start planning a whole room of coordinating items.

roman blind

Roman blinds, with their neat, soft pleats are a sure-fire way to bring seaside chic into your bathroom. That is, assuming that you haven't already turned your bathroom into a wet room.

Use stripes, plain fabrics or fabrics with a small-scale pattern for this project. Larger designs don't give such good results, as the pattern gets lost in the folds. Calling these design decisions yourself is a real luxury and addictively empowering. Bye-bye identikit fabrics and one-size-fits-all … hello craft kitten extraordinaire.

YOU WILL NEED

1   Fabric (read through the first few instructions overleaf to work out measurements)
2   Lining fabric (muslin will do – though wash it first)
3   Wooden batten the width of your blind
4   Wooden lathe (a flat piece of wood the width of your blind that goes in the bottom)
5   Staple gun
6   Blind rings and screw eyes
7   Thin blind cord
8   Acorn (this is a wooden bead to pop all the blind cords through)
9   Cleat (the metal thing you wrap blind strings around)
10 Iron and ironing board
11 Sewing machine and dressmaker's pins
12 Scissors
13 Tape measure

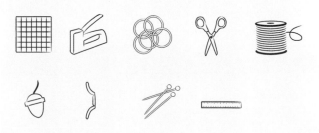

Blinds look best if they fit inside the window recess and are attached to the window frame. You can attach them outside the recess, but they tend to look a little 'stuck on'. Get a friend to hold a sheet up if you need help visualizing what will look best for your window.

Measure the width to the outside edge of the window frame (or the width of the recess, if you intend to attach the blind to the wall). Get your batten cut to this measurement.

Adding a border in contrasting fabric really makes this blind, so although it's a little more hassle it's worth going the extra mile. First you need to calculate your fabric measurements. You have already determined your total blind width; for the total length, measure from the top of the window frame (or recess) to the windowsill. My blind is 47$\frac{1}{2}$ in. wide by 63 in. long.

The border needs to be around 6$\frac{1}{2}$ in. wide to be chunky enough to make a statement. To work out the width of the main

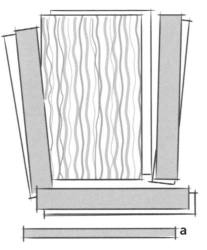

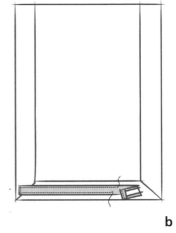

a

b

part of the blind, subtract the width of your border from the width of the finished blind (6$\frac{1}{2}$ in. from each side) and add $\frac{3}{4}$ in. seam allowance to this measurement. This makes the central panel of my blind 35 in. wide.

To calculate the length of the central panel, subtract one border width from your finished blind length and add $\frac{3}{4}$ in. (half seam allowance and half to fold over the top of your batten when you fix the blind to it). (My finished length is 57 in.; I subtracted 6$\frac{1}{2}$ in. from this, giving me 50$\frac{1}{2}$ in., then added $\frac{3}{4}$ in., so the length of the main section of my blind is 51$\frac{1}{4}$ in.)

You now have the length and width of the central panel of your blind. Cut this out in your main fabric, then cut a piece of plain lining fabric to the same size.

Now for the border: add a $\frac{1}{4}$ in. seam allowance on each side to its 6$\frac{1}{2}$ in. width (making it 7$\frac{1}{2}$ in.). The bottom border should be the same width as the finished blind will be plus $\frac{3}{4}$ in. seam allowance. My finished blind is 47$\frac{1}{4}$ + $\frac{3}{4}$ in. = 48 in.

For the border on each side of your blind, cut a piece the same width as your bottom border (7$\frac{1}{2}$ in.) and the length of your finished blind plus $\frac{3}{4}$ in. (half seam allowance and half to fold

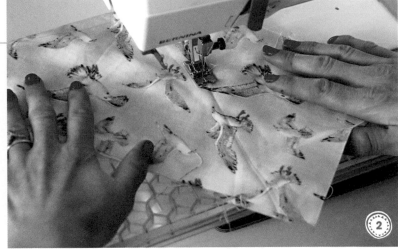

over the top of your batten). Cut out two sets of each border (one for the front and one for the back). Then cut one further bottom border, but make it half the width (3³/4. x 48 in.) (see diagram a). This half-width border is to create a 'sleeve' at the bottom of the blind on the back to pop your wooden lathe into (see diagram b).

Weighting the blind evenly like this makes it hang perfectly straight, rather than folding in at the sides, which is what the material would do naturally.

Stitch the side borders to the central panel and then sew on the bottom border, making sure that the fabrics are right sides together. Stop sewing each seam

1/4 in. from the bottom corners of the blind. Finish with a reverse stitch to secure the seam.

You'll have floppy unstitched fabric left at each corner, which you need to miter. To do this, fold the excess back diagonally and press with an iron. [1]

Place the border fabrics right sides together, match the pressed lines and pin them together. Starting from the inside edge of the border, stitch along the pressed line, reverse-stitching at the start and finish. [2] Cut off the excess fabric and press the seam open so it lies flat. Do this with both corners.

Sew the back borders to the lining in the same way.

Take the 'sleeve' fabric, turn both edges under twice along the length, and press.

Turn both ends of the sleeve under, press and then sew them down.

Pin this sleeve onto the back piece of the blind border, parallel to the bottom of the border and 3/4 in. up from the raw edge. Sew along the top and the bottom, leaving the ends open – this is where you will slot the lathe in, to weight the blind down. Pin the front and back pieces of the blind right sides together and stitch the sides and bottom, 1/4 in. in from the edge. Be sure to keep the raw edges aligned as you sew and leave the top open.

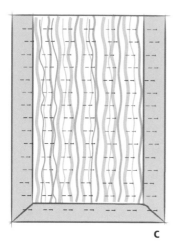

c

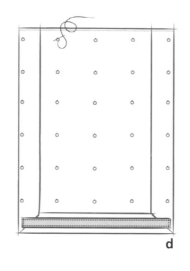

d

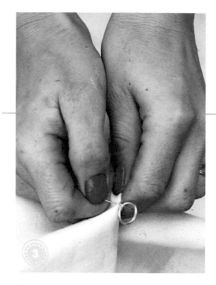

Snip a diagonal line across the bottom corners to trim off the excess fabric.

Turn the blind right side out. Press, and then lay it perfectly flat on the floor. Pin through the front and back pieces at 4 in. intervals, in lines (see diagram c). This is to keep the front and back in exactly the right corresponding place when you stitch the rings onto the back. If you don't do this (which is tempting!) you'll end up with the blind hanging skewed.

Zigzag-stitch the top opening closed, without turning the raw edges under – you do not want to bulk this top bit up with seams as it has to be stapled onto the wooden batten. Besides it'll be at the top and out of sight.

Now you are going to stitch your rings in a grid-like fashion onto the back of the blind (see diagram d). Begin by sewing a line of rings $1/4$ in. in from each side of the blind. Starting from the top, your first ring should be $9^{1}/2$ in. down. Just attach it with a few stitches, then secure your thread with a knot. [3] Stitch another ring every $9^{1}/2$ in., making sure they are perfectly aligned vertically. Stop sewing rings about 10 in. or so from the bottom. You don't want your lovely border folding up with the rest of the blind.

Fold the blind in half lengthways and make marks for hoops on the other side, $1/4$ in. in from the edge, as before. They need to be exactly aligned horizontally, to keep the folds straight.

Divide the middle piece up into equal sections of about $9^{3}/4$ in. each (or however many equal sections will fit between the two sides). Sew a ring every $9^{1}/2$ in. down each section line, exactly in line with the ring above it, as well as on the same horizontal line as the rings on either side.

Fold the top $1/4$ in. of the blind (the edge you have zigzag-stitched) over the top of the batten and staple all the way along with a staple gun.

Fix a screw eye onto the back of the batten at the top of each vertical row of rings. Tie a length of thin cord to the bottom ring in each row. Each of your cords should be double the length of the blind plus the width measurement of the blind.

Thread the cord up through each ring in the row of rings above it until you reach the screw eye at the top. **[4]**

Thread the cord through the screw eye from left to right. Then thread it through all the other screw eyes all the way to the right of the blind.

Once you have all the cords threaded up their respective rows and through all the screw eyes to the one at the far right, pop the cords through the acorn (this is a wooden bead specifically for this purpose). **[5]** You might need to singe the ends of the cords so they're easier to push through the hole in the middle. Make sure all the cords are level so that your blind will draw up evenly, then tie them together in a knot and trim off any excess. The knot should disappear inside the acorn.

Slot the wooden lathe into the sleeve on the back of the blind. **[6]**

Now fix your blind to the window and screw the metal cleat to the left of where your blind is hanging (this is where all your cords will be coming down). Pull the cords by the acorn to raise and lower the blind and wrap the cords around the cleat to hold the blind in your chosen position.

string-covered chair

Forget sloshing tired furniture with white paint. That's over – and as for painting it black, well, that never really happened except in interiors magazines, did it? Instead, consider the possibility of more sensual, textured surfaces. Specifically, natural-looking lumps and bumps that will softly catch the sunlight.

There are a number of ways to achieve the look – a redundant table covered with shells and then topped with glass, or mosaic tiling, which looks stunning on tabletops and chairs; cover the legs, too, and the outcome is fresh and unexpected.

String coiling offers similarly quirky results and is a lot quicker to do. Teamed with shells, coiling offers a much-needed new take on the seaside theme. Think Ralph Lauren beach houses, open windows and a sea breeze. Once you've got into the groove of the methodical looping process, see what else you can apply the same technique to. I chose natural string, but have shown the steps in green to make the process easier to follow.

YOU WILL NEED

1 Chair
2 String, jute or cord (this chair took 55 yards of string)
3 PVA glue
4 Scissors
5 Hammer
6 Tacks
7 Tape measure
8 Fabric scraps for stumps or découpage
9 Shells and fishing line for decoration

METHOD

Cut two lengths of string 5 yards long. Fold both in half, so you have four ends – the four strands you'll be working with. Using four strands at a time makes the process much quicker.

Take the folded point of each of your two pieces of cord and glue firmly to the base of the chair leg, then hammer in a tack to secure. **[1]** Knock another tack into the back of the chair leg, at the bottom, to hook the cords around so you're in the correct position to start winding horizontally around the leg.

Tie the loose ends of the cords into a neat bundle, leaving half a yard or so to work with. Apply glue 2 in. up the chair leg, and start coiling the string around the leg, holding the four strands taut as you do so. **[2]** Make sure you keep the strands parallel (no criss-crossing!) and don't leave any gaps between the coils.

Apply more glue up the leg as you go, and keep the tension firm and even. This is what will give your finished chair a neat and professional finish.

When you get to the top of the leg, tie a knot in the end of each strand, snip off any excess string and secure with a tack at the back. Stagger where you finish each piece of string as there won't be room for all the tacks to finish in the same place.

It's important to use continuous strands for each leg or section of the chair frame (lots of knots at the back will look terrible). Once you have seen how much the first 10 yards will cover, you can estimate how much string you'll need for the other sections of the chair. Do this by eye, or work it out if you are so inclined. For example, I needed 10 yards of string to cover my chair leg. The leg is 13³/₄ in. long. 360 in divided by 13³/₄ in. equals 26.18 in. This means that I will need 26.18 in of string to cover eachy inch of chair (assuming that each part of the chair frame is the same diameter as the leg). Remember to take into account that you are using multiple

Repeat the process to cover the other three chair legs.

Then cover the back in the same way. If you're going to cover the cross member, do this before the sides. This way, you can conceal the ends of the cross section when you wrap the sides.

For the top of each side, either use a contrasting texture – as I did with this striped fabric, which I glued and then tacked in place – or continue with string. To do the latter, cover the top with glue, then coil the string in decreasing circles until the stumps are covered. Glue the end under and secure with a tack in the center.

I strung together a few shells with fishing line to hang from the back and découpaged fabric to the frame. To do this, cut out shapes and glue them on with watered-down glue (70% glue to 30% water). Paint a layer or two of glue over the top and varnish

resin tabletop

Artists and designers have been using synthetic resins in unexpected ways for years – think of Rachel Whiteread's clear resin table and chairs. But why should designers get all the credit when you can create dynamic, personal pieces of your own that will become an enduring keepsake for years to come? You don't need any specific skills, just decorative bits and pieces to set in the resin and the ability to accurately read the side of a measuring jug.

Tabletops are easy to cast and a sleek, playful way of showing off your creativity. The resin makes objects appear as though they're underwater – as if you could put your hand in and grab them. I put a load of jewelery from my teenage years into this table. A little like Lycra after the age of 30, I didn't want to wear it but, unlike Lycra, I couldn't face throwing it out. The pirate's treasure chest idea seemed like it would be a good memorial to years of being a market magpie.

Do this project outside (you need lots of ventilation) and don't involve children in the resin mixing and pouring stages.

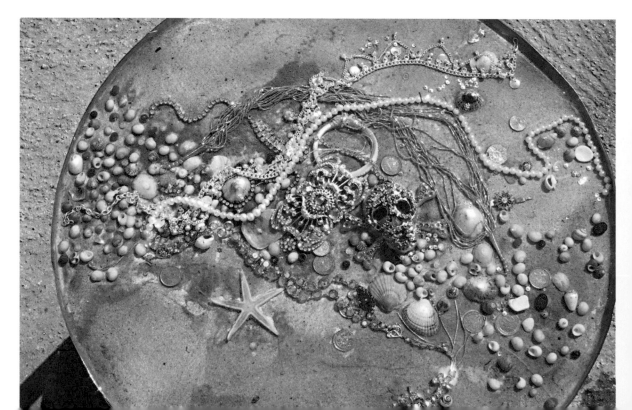

YOU WILL NEED

1 Flat-topped wooden table
2 Copper rim (this will determine the depth of your resin; you don't want to cast any deeper than 3/4 in., so buy a rim 3/4–1 in. wide)
3 Copper nails (you need to use like with like in order to avoid corrosion or the metal going green – there's no glamour in that)
4 Objects to place in the casting (I chose jewellery, shells and sand; you don't want anything that sticks up more than 3/4 in., as they could cause problems like air bubbles and stress lines)
5 2-pack clear cast epoxy resin system (this consists of resin and hardener; like hair dye, these only start to work when you mix them together in specific quantities)
6 Silcone sealant and a sealant gun (available from any hardware or craft store)
7 PVA glue and a piece of stiff card to spread it evenly
8 Gloves and a mask
9 Hammer
10 Dowelling or glass rod to mix the resin and hardener

METHOD

Using copper nails, attach the copper rim all the way around the edge of your tabletop, hammering in one nail about every 3/4 -1 in. [1]
As you're going around the edge, be careful to hold the copper rim completely flush to the edge of the table. You don't want any gaps. The amount that the rim sticks up above the surface of your table is how deep your casting will be. Don't have it any higher than 3/4 in., or the resin will take for ever to set.

177

Clean the tabletop, then apply a coat of PVA glue to seal it, spreading it evenly over the surface using a piece of stiff card or plastic. **[2]** Leave it to dry – you can tell when it's completely dry, as the glue becomes clear.

Squirt a line of clear silicone sealant all the way around where the copper rim joins the tabletop. **[3]** This is to seal any gaps, so when you pour on the resin it won't escape.

Stick your chosen objects onto the tabletop using glue; this is to stop any movement when you pour the resin. **[4]** I chose stacks of jewelery, shells and sand.

You need to do the following in a well-ventilated, dust-free environment that is not inside your home – such as the garden or a garage. Children and pets should be kept well away.

For the best result, use a spirit level and wedge the legs or table base to achieve a flat surface.

Wearing gloves and a mask, mix the resin and hardener, as per the manufacturer's instructions. (Generally this is a ratio of 2 parts resin to 1 part hardener – but do it exactly as instructed.) Stir thoroughly with a clean, dry piece of dowelling or a glass rod (do this for at least five minutes to avoid pockets of unmixed solution – anything unmixed will not set).

Very slowly and carefully, pour the mixture evenly across the tabletop. Leave the table to set.

This will take between one and three days and it's a good idea to erect a cover to protect it from dust during this period. Don't move or touch it, just check it daily by tapping the side gently to see if the surface moves. You should try to keep the environment around 68°–77°F. This resin type takes so long to set that any air pockets that have formed should dissipate on their own, you'll be pleased to hear.

shark doorstop

YOU WILL NEED

1 Plastic mold (available from resin suppliers) or an ice cream tub or similar
2 Plastic toy shark (or another object to place in the casting)
3 Plastic measuring jug
4 PVA release agent
5 Wooden spoon or mixing rod (available from resin suppliers)
6 Fishing line and lollipop stick (or similar)

METHOD

Still got a little resin left over? This tongue-in-cheek doorstop is guaranteed to amuse your friends and confuse your cat.

As with the table (page 176) you'll need to make this outside or in a well-ventilated garage. And ideally the temperature should be 68°–77°F, so grab a fan heater to keep your work warm. Castings that are this thick can crack as they set if they heat up too quickly, so don't lose heart if this takes a couple of goes to get right.

Fill a plastic mold (an ice cream tub or similar) with water and pour it into a plastic measuring jug to determine the quantity of resin and hardener you need. Don't fill the mold completely as the shark will displace some of the resin.

Thoroughly dry the mold and jug. Wipe the inside of the mold with PVA release agent (your resin supplier will sell this); it's like buttering a cake tin and enables you to get your cast out once it's set.

If the mold you are using has a curved bottom, secure it to a base – Plasticine is perfect for this – but prop it up on either side as well. If it slips, you'll have plastic splats all over the floor that won't scrape off.

Wearing gloves and a mask, mix a third of the resin and hardener that you need according to the manufacturer's instructions.

SLOWLY pour this mixture into the plastic mold (working slowly reduces the risk of air bubbles). Leave this until it has nearly set (this will take a day or so).

Now tie one end of a length of fishing line around a toy shark and the other to a lollipop stick, or similar, that you can rest over the top of the mold to suspend the shark. Slowly lower the shark until it rests on the surface of the nearly set resin in the bottom of your mold.

Mix the rest of your resin and hardener and pour over the shark, being careful not to jog the lollipop stick.

Leave the casting to set. This will take about 24 hours.

braided bathmat

Braided rugs have the homespun sensibility of 1960s and 1970s Swedish design, which is very hip right now. This strand of folk art, which dates back to Ancient Egypt and Peruvian times and was a recycling favorite of the first American settlers, is following knitting and weaving as the latest handicraft to shrug off its granny-in-a-rocking-chair image and become the latest expression in homemade chic.

Plaits are so simple to do that I almost want to apologize, and I definitely want to suggest that you enlist the help of children, as I have with Molly. Use scraps of fabric left over from other projects to make a bathmat that matches, or old pieces of clothing and bed linen that will feel delightfully soft underfoot – the effects can be amazing. The process is super-calming, with its rhythmic motion, and it's a great way to revitalize tired but treasured fabric that you just can't bear to throw out, creating a veritable Ferris wheel of braided memories that will swirl under your feet as you hop out of the bath in the morning.

YOU WILL NEED

1 Lots of material (choose fabrics that won't fray or shed their pile; remember that you'll be walking on this, so don't use anything with scratchy metallic fibres – cottons are perfect, as are jerseys and hosiery. You'll need around 4 x 1 yad to make an oval rug of 20 x 16 in.)
2 Large household needle
3 Strong thread (something like carpet thread is ideal)
4 Fabric scissors

METHOD

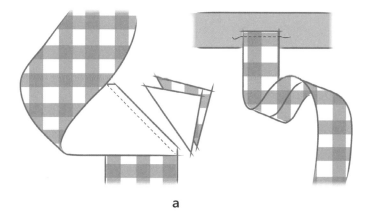 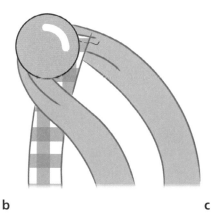

a   b   c

Look at the colors you're working with. If you have one main shade and a few that are completely different, group strands of each color together, so you'll get bands of color in your design. Work out which will look best next to each other in your finished design by coiling up the cut-up strips and placing them next to one another.

Cut your fabric into strips 3 in. wide. If you're working with long pieces of fabric (for example, cut from a sheet), sew two lengths together on the bias (see diagram a) and work with a single length (that is half the length of the two sewn together). If you are using smaller pieces of fabric, sew them together to form two long continuous strips, one half the length of the other.

Iron both sides of the strips under, so they meet in the center. This makes the braiding so much easier and quicker.

Place the shorter of the two strips in the center of the longer strip and stitch the end down at right angles to the center of the long piece, creating a 'T' shape (see diagram b).

Hook this 'T' onto a door handle, so that you have three strands of fabric in front of you (see diagram c). This will keep your hands free for braiding. Alternatively work with a little helper who can hold it. It's worth rolling the long ends into a neat bundle and securing them with an elastic band before you get started to stop them from tangling up as you braid.

Make sure all your strands have the raw edges firmly tucked underneath – you don't want these showing on your finished piece.

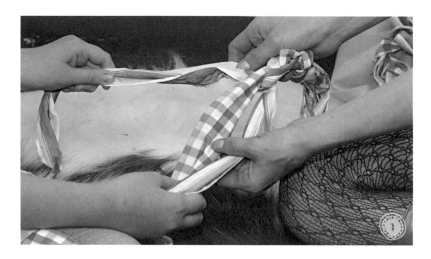

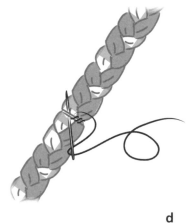

d

You have three strands of fabric in front of you. Take the strand on the left over the middle strand (now this strand is in the middle), then take the strand on your right over this new middle strand. [1] That's your first braid. Now repeat the process. Easy. Just keep going!

Once you've finished braiding one set of strips, secure the ends with a few stitches to prevent the braid from unravelling. Then start another breaid, sewing the end of one short strip to the center of a long strip to create a 'T' shape, as before.

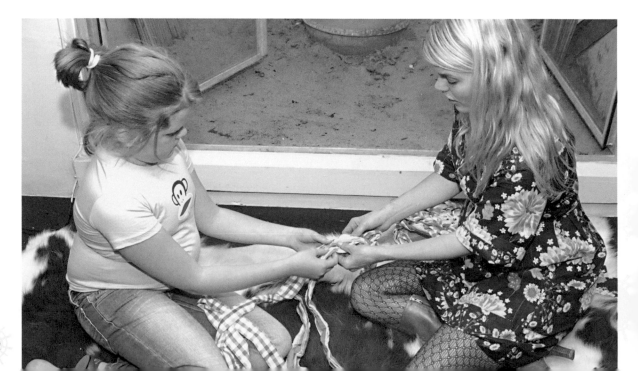

Join the finished braids together by butting up the ends and sewing them together with a few stitches (see diagram d).

When you have a good few yards of braided fabric – say 10 yards – start coiling them into your chosen mat shape and sew them together as you go. If you want a round mat, begin coiling the plait in a tight circle. For an oval mat, place a long straight section of braiding on the floor (12 in. is a good start for an oval mat) and begin coiling your lengths of braid around this.

Your stitches should be big zigzags between the coils. **[2]** Ideally you want to disturb the look of the braid as little as possible, so tuck the needle in wherever the strip is naturally falling, rather than yanking the braids closer together or out of place.

You can sew as many braided strips together as you like, to make the finished piece as big as you wish. When you've decided enough is enough, just fold the ends under, tuck them into the underside of the adjacent coil and secure with a couple of stitches. **[3]**

Garden

the big green room

wind wheel

Wind wheels take only minutes to make and are mesmerizing to watch on blustery days. They're perfect for glamorizing gardens and children will love them, especially if you set them the challenge of drawing patterns on the points. These have the same animated effect as flick books when the wheels spin fast in the wind.

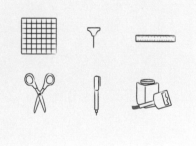

YOU WILL NEED

1   Card (each of these wind wheels was made from a piece of card 12 x 12 in.)
2   Fabric or paper for decoration (or set children the task of drawing pictures)
3   Dowelling
4   Drawing pin and a map pin
5   Small bead
6   Water-based spray mount; try 3M Pro-Spray (do go for a water-based version, as solvent-based adhesives are harmful to your children's health and the environment)
7   Metal ruler
8   Scissors
9   Pen

METHOD

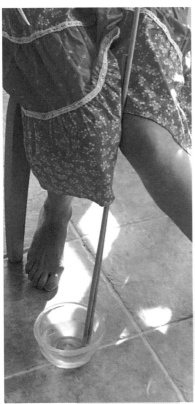

Soak the top end of your dowelling in a bowl of water to make the wood flexible.

Cut a square of card. Wind wheels tend to measure 6¼ in. across or less, but the children I made these ones for decided on 12 in. Supersizing means you'll need a bigger gust of wind to get the wind wheels moving, but, like outsize wallpaper prints, they look marvelous.

Spray the card with spray mount, then place the fabric on top and smooth it flat with your hands. Trim the fabric to the size of your card.

Do the same with the other side of the card, using contrasting fabric or colored paper.

Fold the covered card in half, diagonally, and in half again, then unfold. Using a ruler, mark a point three-quarters of the way to the center on each of the four diagonal creases. Cut along these lines, dividing each corner into two points.

Bring every other point to the center and hold them with your finger. Push the drawing pin through all the layers. Then remove it and put the map pin through the hole. Drawing pins are slightly bigger in diameter than map pins; this minimal slack is what lets the wheel spin. Slip the bead onto the end of the map pin, behind the wind wheel head, then push the pin into the dowelling, ¼–½ in. from the top.

Take your creation outside, run along a beach with it whirling behind or stake it in the garden, so it looks like a giant techni-color sunflower.

painted glasses

Glass painting looks best if it is done quickly, so the least complicated ideas give the most successful results. I've painted a water jug and glasses with a simple parrot design based on a 1960s Josef Frank fabric. The shapes can be filled in with just a few brushstrokes. The paint doesn't dry instantly, so keep tissues to hand – if you mess up, just wipe it off and have another go. Once set, the paint is robust and dishwasher-proof.

YOU WILL NEED

1 Glass jug and glasses
2 Bake-in-the-oven glass paints (the ones I used were from the Pebeo Vitra 160 range)
3 Paintbrush
4 Paper and pen
5 Masking tape or newspaper

METHOD

Wash your glassware in warm soapy water and dry it with a soft lint-free cloth. It needs to be completely clean, dry and free from dust.

Practice painting some lines on an old glass or jar first, to get the hang of it. This way you'll see how the paints work and what each brushstroke will look like. You'll notice that quick, definite strokes look better than dithering, thought-out ones. It's worth getting an idea of this before you begin, so that you can plan an appropriate design.

Decide on your design and draw it out on a piece of paper. If you have a fabric or book with a pattern that you especially like, photocopy it and enlarge or reduce it to a size that suits the glass or jug you are working on.

Slide the paper design inside your glass or jug and secure it with a little masking tape, or use scrunched-up newspaper in the middle to hold it in place, and start painting. **[1 and 2]**

If your paints need thinning, use a thinning agent recommended by the paint supplier – don't assume this will be water (it won't be, unless you are using water-based paints).

Leave the paint to dry for a day, then place the glasses and jug in an oven set at 320°F. Leave them for 40 minutes, then turn the oven off and allow it to cool down gradually before taking the glassware out. It's important that you let it cool slowly, as sudden drops in temperature can cause glass to crack – something that you probably knew already.

party flags

Colorful flags practically screams 'CELEBRATION!', making it perfect for dressing weddings, painting the sky at summer parties and adding cheer to children's birthdays. It's one of the few decorator's tricks that can be used to add color above table and floor height. You can buy ready-made flags, of course, but who wants polyester colored triangles when you can have an array of batik, florals, polka dots and snazzy 1960s prints? Making your own is quick, easy, and gives off an air of devilish domesticity.

Any fabric – even an old sheet – will do, as long as you intersperse the plainer pieces with a couple of 'statement fabrics' to raise the bar. And if you are a collector of fabric, don't miss a trick – this is your opportunity to really show off your collection

and enjoy your friends' admiration of your artistic eye and gorgeous vintage finds, without the hassle of having to do something big, like upholster a chair.

Before you forage for fabric, remember that small patterns that look good close up will be lost at a distance. Crank up your color scheme with neons and opt for big, bold patterns. From a few yards away these will seem as tasteful as they did tacky when they were right under your nose.

Here are two methods – a quick one (if the party is the next day) and a lasting method for flags that you can pull out year after year. Children are ideal helpers for something this easy, so don't bust a gut: start a production line and enjoy the art of delegation.

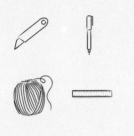

1   Firm card
2   Ruler and pencil
3   Craft knife and cutting mat
4   Pinking shears
5   Garden string
6   Ribbon
AND
7   For the quick method: Sellotape, double-sided tape and craft glue
8   For the longer-lasting method: sewing machine, iron and ironing board

METHOD

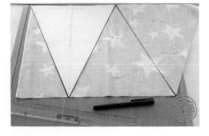

Begin both methods in the same way:

Create a template with some firm card. To do this draw a rectangle 8$^1/_2$ in. wide and 9$^3/_4$ in. long. Mark the center point on one of the 8$^1/_2$ in. lines and draw a line joining this point to the corners of the other 8$^1/_2$ in. line. Cut out your triangle using a craft knife, a ruler and a cutting mat. Put to one side.

Now take your fabric and fold the edge of the fabric over 8$^1/_2$ in. If you like, you can fold it over a few more times to cut more pieces at once. Using the card template, with the base of the triangle aligned with the fold, draw as many triangles (side by side) as will fit along the fold. [1 and 2]

Cut out the triangles using pinking shears.

The quick method

Separate the single triangles from the double-sided flags that have a fold in the top. The ones with the fold are the ones you need for the flags. Now cut a piece of garden string to your chosen length.

Place a length of double-sided tape along the fold on the wrong side of each fabric flag. Remove the tape backing and fold the flag centrally over your garden string. Place a flag about every 12 in. along the string.

Stick the insides of each flag together with craft glue or double-sided tape.

If you have the time or inclination, tie ribbons onto the string in between the flags. Use the leftover single flags to decorate the sides of tables or any surface on which only one side will show. Just cut a piece of string long enough to go around whatever it is that you are decorating, place Sellotape along the top edge of each flag, fold it over the string and back on itself to secure. Then tie to the table. This is a great quick-fix décor idea for weddings.

The longer-lasting method

As above, cut out triangle shapes using your template, but add a ¼ in. seam allowance all the way around and cut along the fold line so you have lots of one-sided flags.

Place the right sides of two triangles together and sew around the 'V' shape. **[3]** Use like fabrics for each flag – with light streaming through you'll see both patterns at the same time if you mix and match, which will look muddled.

Snip off the excess fabric across the point of the triangle, close to the seam. Turn the flag right side out and press it flat with an iron. **[4]**

Fold the cut top edges to the inside of the triangle and press them to neaten. Pin the string along this edge and zigzag-stitch the lot together. Sew on more flags in the same way, leaving a space the size of one and a half flags between them. Finally, tie on the ribbons at intervals.

Now dust down the barbecue and dig out your favorite summer cookbooks – you have parties to plan.

batik cocktail trolley

Once you've bought your outdoor table and chairs, a trolley should be your next purchase. With large flat surfaces, they're ideal for serving afternoon teas (stacked with delicious cakes) or barbecue food, or for being wheeled around at al fresco parties, jangling with glasses of candy-colored cocktails. In fact, it's a wonder that any garden-owning girl worth her salt has ever lived without one.

Trolleys are easy to pick up from junk shops. Choose one with a shape you like and a surface that you can stick to – wood is ideal but plastics and metal are also fine. Don't worry about its condition – you're covering it anyway. Then dig around in thrift stores and at flea markets for some bright clashy cloth, like the natty batik fabrics I used here.

YOU WILL NEED

1 Trolley (Wooden ones can be found anywhere and are ideal for sticking fabric to; alternatively, a chrome or metal trolley is fine. Mine was a support trolley from a nursing home, so let's hope the granny that used it approves of its transformation.)

2 Fabric (Go for the wildest fabrics you can find. I chose batiks in different colors. Keep to one style of fabric, or choose colors that match or clash well.)

3 Sandpaper and a soft cloth (to wipe the wood down after sanding)

4 Paint and paintbrush (if you want to paint the wooden frame)

5 Paper, such as newspaper (for making a pattern), and pins

6 Scissors

7 Iron and ironing board

8 Double-sided tape

9 PVA glue

10 Piece of thin card (for spreading the glue)

11 Clear craft sealer (such as Plasti-kote)

12 Acrylic sealer and paintbrush

If your trolley is wooden or plastic, sand it lightly and then wipe it down with a soft cloth. If your trolley is metal, just wipe it clean of any dust.

Choose your fabrics. Stick to thin cotton, which absorbs glue; thick fabric will make your trolley look mummified. If you're not sure what matches, a couple of ground rules to follow are: 1) go for any color you want, but in the same style of pattern (as I did with these batiks); 2) pick colors that work together (get inspiration from the collections of designers who know best, like Marni) and use any patterns you like. Lay all of your fabrics out and edit them down according to which sit well together, now that you have them all in one place.

Select the fabrics you want to use to cover the shelves first. At this point, decide whether you want to cover the rest of the trolley with fabric, too. Metal or chrome frames are often better left uncovered, while wooden frames can look great painted. Bear in mind that covering only the shelves will be less work, but if you're after something really wild, you simply have to cover the whole thing.

If you've decided to paint the frame, do it now before you start glueing fabric down. Choose a color that suits your fabrics (picking the darkest color from one of the patterns is a good rule of thumb); remember to buy paint appropriate for the surface (you can easily buy wood, metal and melamine paints from any craft store). Apply two coats, leaving it to dry thoroughly between coats.

Cut a key for the shelves – this is a piece of paper that is the exact size and shape of each of the trolley shelves. You can use any paper for this – newspaper, letter photocopy paper, whatever. Stick more than one piece together (if necessary) and trim down until you have a piece that exactly matches the shelf, including indents where the legs join. Do this for each shelf.

If you're going to use the trolley regularly, consider getting glass cut to protect the shelves – this will make dealing with spillages much easier.

Pin the paper patterns to the fabric, making sure that any design on the fabric is the right way round for how you want it to appear on the shelf. Cut 1/8 in. outside the pattern all the way round. With the pattern still attached, iron the 1/8 in. of fabric over the edge of the paper, so it's the right size for the shelf but without raggy edges. For the indents (if there are any), cut a slit in the 1/8 in. excess at the points where the corner or curve falls – this will

allow the fabric the flexibility to be pressed round the corners. Remove the pattern and check that the fabric fits the shelf correctly. Run a thin line of PVA under the fold around the edge and glue it down. Repeat for the other shelves.

Leaving the backing on, place double-sided tape around the four edges of each shelf. Using a piece of card, smear a thin layer of PVA across the rest of the shelf. Remove the tape backing and gently lay the fabric down, smoothing it out from the center with your hands to remove any wrinkles and air bubbles. **[1]**

If you want to cover the legs of the trolley with fabric, too, cut two strips of fabric, a little longer than the legs and just over half the circumference. Smear a thin layer of glue onto the leg with card, press one strip of fabric around one half of the leg, then press the other strip in place. Overlap the join slightly and use scissors to snip away the excess fabric. **[2 and 3]**

For the stumps at the top of each leg, employ the same technique as for making a dart in a piece of clothing. Smear glue over the whole area you want to cover. Glue a rectangle of cloth halfway around the stump with the excess length sticking up. Press it down, pinching out the surplus fabric, then trim it off. **[4]** Do the same for the other half of the stump, hold the sides and top firmly in place until the glue has set. **[5]**

Spray your entire trolley with clear craft sealer (Plasti-kote do a good one, available in craft stores nationwide). For extra protection, paint on an acrylic sealer (available from hardware stores). Just dab a small amount onto your paintbrush – you don't want to soak it.

mosaic table

One look at Gaudí's extraordinary mosaic sculptures in Park Güell, Barcelona, or a stumble across a 1930s tiled courtyard in the Californian or Mexican desert, and you'll want to know how to mosaic. It's a timeless craft that you can make as modern or as traditional as the materials and patterns that you choose.

A table is a good place to start. It's a contained area (and therefore easy to plan) and a little like doing a jigsaw puzzle at Christmas, only you're making the pieces to fit. It's fun to do with friends or family and the finished design, with all its quirks, will bear the 'signature' of the makers – a physical reminder of time spent creating, gossiping and bonding with loved ones. My mother, however, who worked with me until the early hours on a few nights on this particular table, may beg to differ on these points.

As a table requires a flat surface, you will need to use the indirect method. This means that you will create the design in reverse on some brown paper and then transfer it onto the tabletop. This method has advantages over sticking the tiles straight on: you'll see the pattern develop as you go along (giving you more time to rectify mistakes), and the final surface will be completely flat – a necessity if you ever want to place a glass on it.

Start by finding a table to mosaic on – perhaps revive a piece you already have – the only requirement is a smallish flat surface. Then work out a design. As long as you steer clear of the usual motifs, such as anything you see in craft stores, mosaic is perfect for making a statement piece. Think of things you'd like in your garden – insects, tropical fish, birds of paradise or an abstract pattern – but don't rush the design process.

I used a table that my mother had bought years ago. We spent months discussing a Missoni-like zigzag but never got round to buying the tiles. Two years passed and she decided on a dragonfly. Then my father produced a book of jungle scenes by Henri Rousseau. Perfect for adding punchy colors to my parents' increasingly tropical-looking conservatory. Half the fun is enjoying the natural pace of the creative process, so don't just go with your initial idea.

This table took us three days. We worked at quite a pace and my normally genteel mother swore fruitily on three occasions. So, if this is your first attempt, choose a simpler design or an abstract pattern using mainly whole tiles, for example – or use a smaller table.

On the subject of size, large projects don't require more skill, but they take longer and are marginally more complicated when fixing the tiles to the adhesive, as you need to cut the pattern into pieces, because the tiles will be too heavy to flip over in one.

YOU WILL NEED

1   Small table (revamp an old one or make one using marine ply)
2   Copper rim $1/4$–$3/4$ in. deep and the circumference of your table, copper nails and a hammer
3   Mosaic tiles (Venetian glass tiles are your best bet. They're easiest to cut and come in every color under the sun.)
4   Heavy-duty tile nippers
5   Tile grout (use different colors to accent parts of your pattern, or stick to a light sand and darker natural shade, such as charcoal)
6   Firm plastic grout spreader
7   Roll of brown paper and scissors
8   Masking tape, pencil and black marker pen
9   PVA glue and an old jar
10 $1/4$ inch-wide paintbrush
11 Adhesive (if you are working on a wood surface, ask for a flexible adhesive, as wood expands and contracts)
12 Safety goggles and a dust mask
13 Sponge
14 Yacht varnish (if your table is wooden)

Plan your design. This is the fun bit and mosaic tiling is delightfully escapist, so really go to town. Find images that you like the shape of, such as insects, tropical palms or huge vibrant polka dots. Use a photocopier to enlarge them to a suitable size for your table.

Transfer the outline of these shapes onto a large sheet of brown paper with a pencil. This is easy – tape your images to a window and place the brown paper over the top. The daylight will shine through, allowing you to trace the outlines. It's important that you use brown paper, as this is strong enough to hold the tiles, whereas normal paper is not.

Once you've drawn a basic outline, go over your pencil lines with a big black marker pen. Mosaic is a bold craft, so simplify intricacies at thispoint. [1]

Cut the paper with the design on it to the exact size of the surface you are covering. You need to be exact. Any bigger and it won't fit; any smaller and you'll be left with big patches of grout.

Put your safety goggles on. [2] When cutting tiles, chips fly off in all directions. Also, when you're cutting tiles and mixing grout and adhesive, wear a dust mask to stop you from inhaling microscopic particles of ceramic, glass, grout and cement.

In an old jar, mix equal parts of PVA glue with water. It's best to make up just a little at a time – $1/2$ in. in the bottom of the jar will be fine.

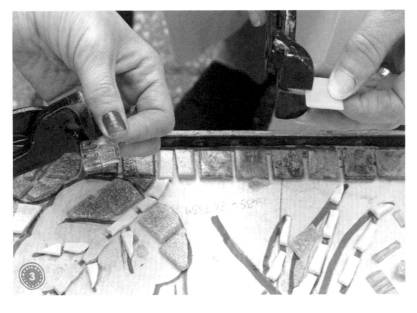

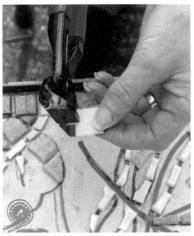

Look at both sides of the tiles before you start sticking them onto the paper. Often, but not always, one side of the tile will be bumpy and the other side will be flat. Remember that they need to be stuck flat side down (this is the side that will show on your finished mosaic).

The next step is to start filling in your design. The order to work in Is as follows: stick an outline of tiles all the way around the edge first, then fill in the main pattern, and finally get to work on the background. [3] To stick the tiles down, paint the flat side of each tile with a little of the PVA mixture. Don't use too much glue – you'll need to peel the paper off eventually to reveal the finished mosaic. Once the glue is dry, the paper and mosaic sheet is very robust.

Whole tiles should suffice for the outline, but when you get on to your main pattern you'll need to cut the tiles into shapes. Practice this first, before you get stuck in. To cut the tiles in order to create shapes other than squares, just place the edge of the tile a close to the jaw of your tile nippers and squeeze. [4] Placing your hands further down the nipper handles gives more leverage. The tile will break in line with the nipper jaws. The more tiles you cut, the easier this will become.

Continue cutting tiles and sticking them right side down until your pattern is complete. **[5]**

Nail a copper rim around the edge of your tabletop. The depth of the rim needs to be $1/4 - 3/4$ in. (deep enough for the adhesive and tiles). Nails should be hammered in about every $3/4$ in.

If your table is wood, seal the surface by painting it with three coats of waterproof yacht varnish, letting it dry between coats. This stops the wood from warping when you place adhesive on it (which will leave you with a bumpy surface). Alternatively, you could make your own table-top using marine ply, which is pre-treated and perfect for mosaic.

If your design is large, the paper will tear under the weight of all the tiles and grout, so snip the design into sections before you start grouting. Use natural breaks in the pattern for cutting lines. You can scribble numbers on the back of the paper to help you position the pieces correctly on the tabletop.

The following needs to be done quickly, as grout and adhesive are only workable for about forty minutes. Mix up the grout and adhesive separately, according to the manufacturer's instructions. Then, using a plastic grout spreader or your fingers, spread grout over the tiles. **[6,7]** Aim to grout between the tiles only, and wipe the backs clean with a damp cloth once you've

finished.

Continue in this way until you have grouted all of the various sections of your design. I used two different colors of grouting – light sand and charcoal – to highlight different parts of my design and add another decorative dimension. **[8]**

Spread an even layer of adhesive on the tabletop. Go right up to the copper rim. **[9]**

The next step is to flip your tile design over and place it on top of the adhesive, so the brown paper is facing up. Make sure you lay each section of the design in its correct position and place it down firmly, but don't squash it hard. **[10]**

When the adhesive has fully set – leaving it overnight is fine – wipe over the paper with a wet sponge. **[11]** The water will soak through the paper, dissolving the glue, so the paper can be pulled away to reveal the mosaic underneath. Peel the paper off really carefully, as any stubborn glue will pull tiles up with it. **[12]**

The tiles will now be embedded in the adhesive, but there will be a few gaps in the grouting between the separate sections of the design. Mix up some more grout and fill these in on the right side of your mosaic. Wipe away any excess grout from the surface with a damp cloth, then leave to dry thoroughly.

decorative tiles

Add a homely feel to your big green room by revitalizing old tiles with eccentric prints. Extending textile or rug patterns, which you'd expect to see inside, past the kitchen door gives them a new context, breaking traditional room boundaries and adding fluidity to the indoor and outdoor spaces of your home.

I transferred the designs of vintage West African and Indian batik fabric onto reclaimed terracotta floor tiles. A lively pattern instantly puts the groove back into gloomy gardens, and these tiles are ideal if you're too lazy for the upkeep of a lawn and flowerbeds.

YOU WILL NEED _____

1 Lightly glazed terracotta tiles – these are from Fired Earth (for unglazed tiles use the turpentine method described on pages 76-78)
2 Lazertran 'Waterslide' transfer paper for photocopiers (Lazertran paper can be a little more expensive than other brands, but it works better than any others I have tried and doesn't tear so easily)
3 Scissors
4 Squeegee
5 Floor varnish and paintbrush

METHOD

Take a photo of the image you want on your tiles and print it onto the shiny side of Lazertran 'Waterslide' paper in reverse, using a color photocopier.

Put the printed sheet in a hot oven for 60–90 seconds to ensure the toners have fused. You'll be able to tell when this has happened as the colors brighten slightly and the paper will appear shinier than before. This prevents air bubbles from forming later on.

Cut the image to size and lower it into clean, lukewarm water for a couple of minutes. When the sheet of backing paper has loosened, carefully slide it off.

Gently remove the transfer from the water. It will be very delicate – like tissue – so be careful not to tear it. Place the transfer face down on your tile and wipe away any moisture or gum – if left, this will go brown during the baking process.

Using a squeegee or your hands gently smooth the air bubbles from center outwards. [1] Don't be surprised if this takes you a couple of tries, due to tearing.

Place your tile in the bottom of a domestic oven at the lowest possible heat for 30 minutes.

Increase the temperature very slightly and leave it in for a further 45 minutes. Increase the temperature every 10 to 15 minutes until the surface of the tile becomes shiny. This will happen at about 400°F (200°C) Since domestic ovens – especially fan-assisted ones – aren't particularly accurate, look at the transfer for guidance, rather than your oven temperature.

To protect the transferred image, apply a few layers of floor varnish suitable for outside use, leaving it to dry completely in between coats. [2]

mirror screen

Add a little theater to your garden with a riotously colorful screen. Placing something normally associated with indoors outdoors may seem odd at first, but the principle is the same. You're either creating a division or covering up something unsightly – and a screen is an arresting medium for splashing a photo or painting across. Here I have had a large-scale color print of an artist's work fixed to a metallic background – hence the luminescence. This in turn was fixed to plywood to create the screen. A far more stylish view than next door's washing line.

You don't even need to get your hands dirty. Just choose an image you love and leave the rest to experts (large-scale printing requires professional equipment). Without the hassle of construction, you'll find yourself free to be more creative. Look through photo albums, magazines and catalogues to find images close to your heart. And don't assume that if you see a picture in a gallery it's off limits – artists and photographers are often happy to negotiate a single-usage fee for their work. Just ask the gallery to contact the artist's agent and they'll suggest a price (it's worth haggling); the principle is no different to downloading a song onto your iPod.

I paid Amazonian artist Elvis Luna $395 to reproduce his jungle sunset painting. I then sent the image to a specialist company, Learn to Dream, for them to print it onto a screen. Now, instead of my neighbor's smalls flapping in the breeze, I see parrots, lashings of foliage and a peach melba sunset out of my kitchen window. Doing the washing-up is (almost) a pleasure.

yoga mats

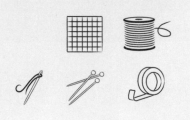

Anyone who thinks that yoga is only about moving onto a higher spiritual plane is in for a shock when they see the higher material plane that much of the kit belongs on. The price tag of serenity, these days, is enough to give you bad energy and a worse credit rating.

OK, it's not so bad if you want a regular sticky mat, but nowadays dressing for yoga is a competition sport. And if your classmates have mini sheepskins or mats made of sari material, then frankly, who cares if you can do square breathing in the double lotus?

But make your own mat and you can dictate the specifications, the look and the eco-friendly materials that you use, without paying the spirituality premium. You'll have perfect body-mat synergy and lose the gut in a week. Well, maybe that's going a bit far, but you'll certainly be pleased with yourself every time you relax into a downward dog – all for an hour's work. Make another for your yogi friend at the same time; it will only take a few minutes more, yet pay enormous karmic dividends.

YOU WILL NEED

1 ½ in.-thick foam, cut to the size you want your mat to be
2 Fabric (something thick, like this Liberty upholstery fabric)
3 Thread to match
4 Needle and sewing machine
5 Pins
6 Large tapestry needle and tapestry thread
7 Iron and ironing board
8 Tailor's chalk
9 Tape measure and set square

METHOD

Work out how large you want your mat to be and get your foam supplier to cut the foam to size when you buy. (Don't be tempted to cut it yourself or it'll look like a dog has chewed it.)

Cut two pieces of fabric $1/2$ in. larger all round than the piece of foam.

Place the right sides of the fabric together and pin.

Starting 4 in. above the bottom corner of one of the long sides, sew around the other sides of the cover, stitching $1/4$ in. in from the edge. (You want to make the cover slightly smaller than the foam, so the fit is snug.) Only sew up about $19^1/2$ in. of the last (long) side, leaving a big enough

hole to slip the foam inside the cover. (It doesn't work if you leave the hole in one of the shorter sides of the cover, as it's too much fuss feeding the foam through.)

Diagonally snip off the excess fabric at each corner, close to the seam. Turn the cover right side out and press with an iron.

Slip the foam through the hole and into the cover, easing it into the corners and making sure it's completely flat, so that the cover doesn't skew when you sew over it.

Turn the raw edges to the inside and hand-sew the hole closed, using slip stitch. Secure with a knot and a few extra slip stitches

at each end (see page 125).

Divide the length of the mat into six or seven equal sections and mark these using tailor's chalk and a set square (so you don't find your stitches going off at an angle).

Thread a tapestry needle with tapestry thread. Using big stab stitches (each stitch can be about $1/4$ in. long), hand-sew across the mat, along the chalk lines that you've marked, stitching right through the foam and out the other side. Secure the thread at each end with a neat knot and trim the excess thread off. These lines of stitches enable your new mat to concertina. Rolling is so last season.

resources

ART AND GRAPHICS

Most local art shops are great for basics. Also, check on line for unusual items.

www.dickblick.com – Graphic, art and technical drawing materials, Pantone guides, and all sorts of papers.

www.colorguides.net – Pantone color guides, textile paper and Pantone software.

BLINDS

American Blinds – Slick blinds in a range of textures and cloths.
(www.decoratetoday.com)

CRAFT SUPPLIERS

Check out your local craft store. To find one near you, go to www.craftsitedirectory.com. This is also a good source for online crafts.

TOOLS

Black and Decker (www.blackanddecker.com)

HARDWARE STORES

www.thinklocal.com is a great directory for stores near you.

THRIFT STORES

www.thethriftshopper.com is a good resource to find thrift stores and consignment stores near you.

RECYCLING

Craigslist – Noticeboard of wanted/unwanted furniture and electrical goods.
(www.craigslist.com)

Recycler's World – Site explaining how and where to recycle and reuse fridges, furniture, mobile phones, car tires, computers, etc.
(www.recycle.net)

SEWING MACHINES

Bernina – Head and shoulders above other makes of machine in terms of quality and lifespan; all machines are still made in Switzerland with metal rather than plastic components. Accessories and models suitable for computer-aided embroidery and good after-care service – a worthwhile investment that all seamstresses, patchworkers and embroiderers swear by.
(www.bernina.com)

Most fabric and quilt stores carry sewing machines, as does department stores. Always feel free to 'test drive' a sewing machine. Remember that you do not have to spend a fortune to find a good sewing machine that meets your needs.

AUCTION HOUSES

Try the big three for their twentieth-century sales – you can often pick up great designer furniture for less than antique dealer prices.
www.bonhams.com, www.christies.com, www.sothebys.com

For local auctions and antiques fairs look in local newspaper listings

ONLINE AUCTIONS

www.ebay.com – The biggest and still the best. You can get practically anything here, as long as you can get it home.

www.shopgoodwill.com – auctions off items from Goodwill stores.

CRAFTS FAIRS

For local craft fairs look in local newspaper listings, or go to www.craftsfaironline.com

MARKETS IN THE USA

There's a huge appetite for markets and garage sales in the US – www.fleamarketguide.com provides up-to-date listings from town to town in every state.

Two markets that I loved in California are:
Rose Bowl Flea Market (www.pasadena.com) – Old surf boards, comic books, Mexican tiles and bric-a-brac. 1001 Rose Bowl Drive, Pasadena, CA, 91103. The second Sunday of each month, 9am–3pm.

San Jose Flea Market (www.sjfm.com) – For arts and crafts, jewellery, tools, furniture, even live music. 12000 Berryessa Road, San Jose, CA. Wednesday–Sunday, 6am–4pm.

A once-a-year garage sale not to miss:
127 Sale (www.tourdekalb.com/yardsale.htm) – The world's longest yard sale runs from Gadsden, AL to Covington, KY. The 4-day event begins the Thursday before the first Saturday in August.

MARKETS IN CANADA

Great web site for listing thrift stores, fairs, and garage/yard sales, www.localyardsales.com/

For an auction house directory go to www.worldartantiques.com/canadaAuctionHouses.htm

MARKETS IN THE UK

New Caledonian Antiques and Flea Market (also known as Bermondsey market) – Great for cut-price antiques, but get there early.
Tube: London Bridge. Fridays, 5am–noon

Portobello Road Market – Like Notting Hill, ultra fashionable, pretty expensive but intriguing stuff from antiques (the south end of the street) to fruit and veg (the middle) to bric-a-brac and clothing (the north end). Early morning on Fridays is when the trade and fashion designers tend to go, probably when you're most likely to get a bargain.
Tube: Notting Hill Gate. Fridays, Saturdays, 7am–4pm (ish)

Spitalfields – Boho weekend market with a burgeoning local artists' community.
Tube: Liverpool Street. Sundays only, 10am–4.30pm

Stables Market, Camden Lock – Furniture by classic and contemporary designers, vintage clothing and collectables.
Tube: Chalk Farm. Friday–Sunday, 10am–6pm

Sunbury Antiques Market, Kempton Park – Furniture and other outsize objects outside; smaller bits and pieces indoors.
Kempton Park Racecourse, 2nd and last Tuesday of the month, 6.30am–1pm

FURTHER AFIELD

www.sable.co.uk and www.shortcitybreak.co.uk list markets across Europe. Plan a road trip.

Some of my favorites are:
Budapest, Hungary
Ecseri Piac
Crystal, porcelain, antique jewellery, embroidery, lace, old toys and all sorts of bric-a-brac.
XIX Nagykorosi ut 156, Monday–Friday, Sunday, 8am–4pm, Saturday 7am–3pm. Tel +1 282 9563

Paris, France
Les Puces de Saint-Ouen
Huge internationally renowned market that sells everything from 'proper antiques' to bric-a-brac.
Metro: Clignancourt. Saturday, Sunday, Monday, 10am–6pm. www.antikita.com

Puces de Vanves
Metro: Porte de Vanves. Saturday and Sunday, 2pm–7.30pm (new goods sector), 7am–7.30pm (second-hand goods sector).

Lille, France
Braderie Annual Street Fair
On the first weekend in September, the city becomes a gigantic flea market with more than 200km of pavements packed with people selling paintings, antiques, ornaments, furniture and junk of every description. Go early, even by 11am it's packed.

Lisbon, Portugal

Brocante du Parque das Nacoes

Favorite second-hand market, similar to the tail
end of Portobello.

Pavilhao do Portugal. 2nd and 3rd Sunday of each
month, 10am–7pm.

Madrid, Spain

El Rastro

Madrid's largest, most popular market selling
everything from second-hand shoes to lampshades,
jewelery, gaudy door knockers, hand-embroidered
cloth and furniture.

Metro: La Latina. Sunday, 7am–3pm.

EVEN FURTHER AFIELD

Thailand

Bangkok, Chatuchak Weekend Market

Skytrain: Mo Chit Station

Thai silks, particularly good for Thai handicrafts
and linens, furniture and household products.
Saturday and Sunday, 9am–6pm. (Friday is a
wholesalers' market 9am–6pm, though it's still OK
to shop there.)

Hong Kong

"Cat Street" off Hollywood Road in Central

Flea market offering inexpensive trinkets, bric-a-
brac, fabric. The neighboring area is famous for
fine arts and antiques. Market are open daily
10am- 7pm

If you'd like to keep up with what Danielle is up to and try a few more projects, log on to **www.houseproudcraft.com**.

Get inspired and email in photos of your own work ... join the new craft revolution!

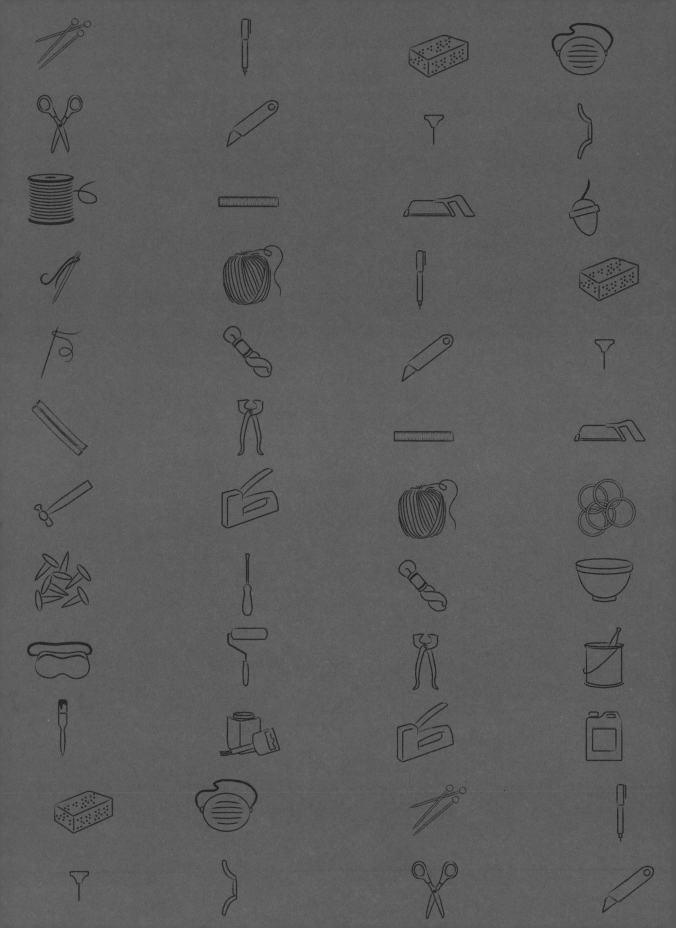